WITH SKILFUL HAND

MCGILL-QUEEN'S STUDIES IN THE HISTORY OF RELIGION

Volumes in this series have been supported by the Jackman Foundation of Toronto.

SERIES TWO   In memory of George Rawlyk
Donald Harman Akenson, Editor

1 Marguerite Bourgeoys and Montreal, 1640–1665
   Patricia Simpson

2 Aspects of the Canadian Evangelical Experience
   G.A. Rawlyk, editor

3 Infinity, Faith, and Time
   Christian Humanism and Renaissance Literature
   John Spencer Hill

4 The Contribution of Presbyterianism to the Maritime provinces of Canada
   Charles H.H. Scobie and G.A. Rawlyk, editors

5 Labour, Love, and Prayer
   Female Piety in Ulster Religious Literature, 1850–1914
   Andrea Ebel Brozyna

6 The Waning of the Green
   Catholics, the Irish, and Identity in Toronto, 1887–1922
   Mark G. McGowan

7 Religion and Nationality in Western Ukraine
   The Greek Catholic Church and the Ruthenian National Movement in Galicia, 1867–1900
   John-Paul Himka

8 Good Citizens
   British Missionaries and Imperial States, 1870–1918
   James G. Greenlee and Charles M. Johnson, editors

9 The Theology of the Oral Torah
   Revealing the Justice of God
   Jacob Neusner

10 Gentle Eminence
   A Life of George Bernard Cardinal Flahiff
   P. Wallace Platt

11 Culture, Religion, and Demographic Behaviour
   Catholics and Lutherans in Alsace, 1750–1870
   Kevin McQuillan

12 Between Damnation and Starvation
   Priests and Merchants in Newfoundland Politics, 1745–1855
   John P. Greene

13 Martin Luther, German Saviour
   German Evangelical Theological Factions and the Interpretation of Luther, 1917–1933
   James M. Stayer

14 Modernity and the Dilemma of North American Anglican Identities, 1880–1950
   William Katerberg

15 The Methodist Church on the Prairies, 1896–1914
   George Emery

16 Christian Attitudes Towards the State of Israel
   Paul Charles Merkley

17 A Social History of the Cloister
   Daily Life in the Teaching Monasteries of the Old Regime
   Elizabeth Rapley

18 Households of Faith
   Family, Gender, and Community in Canada, 1760–1969
   Nancy Christie, editor

19 Blood Ground
   Colonialism, Missions, and the
   Contest for Christianity in the
   Cape Colony and Britain,
   1799–1853
   Elizabeth Elbourne

20 A History of Canadian Catholics
   Gallicanism, Romanism,
   and Canadianism
   Terence J. Fay

21 Archbishop Stagni's Reports
   on the Ontario Bilingual Schools
   Question, 1915
   John Zucchi,   translator and editor

22 The Founding Moment
   Church, Society, and the
   Constructing of Trinity College
   William Westfall

23 The Holocaust, Israel, and
   Canadian Protestant Churches
   Haim Genizi

24 Governing Charities
   Church and State in Toronto's
   Catholic Archdiocese,
   1850–1950
   Paula Maurutto

25 Anglicans and the Atlantic World
   High Churchmen, Evangelicals, and
   the Quebec Connection
   Richard W. Vaudry

26 Evangelicals and the Continental
   Divide: The Conservative Protestant
   Subculture in Canada and the United
   States
   Sam Reimer

27 Christians in a Secular World
   The Canadian Experience
   Kurt Bowen

28 Anatomy of a Séance
   A History of Spirit Communication
   in Central Canada
   Stan McMullin

29 With Skilful Hand
   The Story of King David
   David T. Barnard

SERIES ONE
G.A. Rawlyk, Editor

1 Small Differences
  Irish Catholics and Irish Protestants,
  1815–1922
  An International Perspective
  Donald Harman Akenson

2 Two Worlds
  The Protestant Culture of
  Nineteenth-Century Ontario
  William Westfall

3 An Evangelical Mind
  Nathanael Burwash and the
  Methodist Tradition in Canada,
  1839–1918
  Marguerite Van Die

4 The Dévotes
  Women and Church in
  Seventeenth-Century France
  Elizabeth Rapley

5 The Evangelical Century
  College and Creed in English
  Canada from the Great Revival
  to the Great Depression
  Michael Gauvreau

6 The German Peasants' War and
  Anabaptist Community of Goods
  James M. Stayer

7 A World Mission
Canadian Protestantism and the
Quest for a New International
Order, 1918–1939
Robert Wright

8 Serving the Present Age
Revivalism, Progressivism, and the
Methodist Tradition in Canada
Phyllis D. Airhart

9 A Sensitive Independence
Canadian Methodist Women
Missionaries in Canada and
the Orient, 1881–1925
Rosemary R. Gagan

10 God's Peoples
Covenant and Land in South Africa,
Israel, and Ulster
Donald Harman Akenson

11 Creed and Culture
The Place of English-Speaking
Catholics in Canadian Society,
1750–1930
*Terrence Murphy and Gerald Stortz,
editors*

12 Piety and Nationalism
Lay Voluntary Associations and the
Creation of an Irish-Catholic
Community in Toronto, 1850–1895
Brian P. Clarke

13 Amazing Grace
Studies in Evangelicalism in
Australia, Britain, Canada, and the
United States
*George Rawlyk and Mark A. Noll,
editors*

14 Children of Peace
W. John McIntyre

15 A Solitary Pillar
Montreal's Anglican Church and
the Quiet Revolution
John Marshall

16 Padres in No Man's Land
Canadian Chaplains and
the Great War
Duff Crerar

17 Christian Ethics and Political
Economy in North America
A Critical Analysis of U.S. and
Canadian Approaches
P. Travis Kroeker

18 Pilgrims in Lotus Land
Conservative Protestantism
in British Columbia, 1917–1981
Robert K. Burkinshaw

19 Through Sunshine and Shadow
The Woman's Christian Temperance
Union, Evangelicalism, and Reform
in Ontario, 1874–1930
Sharon Cook

20 Church, College, and Clergy
A History of Theological Education
at Knox College, Toronto, 1844–1994
Brian J. Fraser

21 The Lord's Dominion
The History of Canadian Methodism
Neil Semple

22 A Full-Orbed Christianity
The Protestant Churches and Social
Welfare in Canada, 1900–1940
Nancy Christie and Michael Gauvreau

23 Evangelism and Apostasy
The Evolution and Impact of
Evangelicals in Modern Mexico
Kurt Bowen

24 The Chignecto Covenanters
A Regional History of Reformed
Presbyterianism in New Brunswick
and Nova Scotia, 1827–1905
Eldon Hay

25 Methodists and Women's Education
in Ontario, 1836–1925
Johanna M. Selles

26 Puritanism and Historical
Controversy
William Lamont

With Skilful Hand
The Story of King David

DAVID T. BARNARD

McGill-Queen's University Press
Montreal & Kingston · London · Ithaca

© McGill-Queen's University Press 2004
ISBN 0-7735-2714-1

Legal deposit second quarter 2004
Bibliothèque nationale du Québec

Printed in Canada on acid-free paper that is 100% ancient forest free (100% post-consumer recycled), processed chlorine free.

McGill-Queen's University Press acknowledges the support of the Canada Council for the Arts for our publishing program. We also acknowledge the financial support of the Government of Canada through the Book Publishing Industry Development Program (BPIDP) for our publishing activities.

The scripture quotations contained herein are from the *New Revised Standard Version Bible*, copyright ©1989 by the Division of Christian Education of the National Council of Churches of Christ in the U.S.A., and are used by permission. All rights reserved.

National Library of Canada Cataloguing in Publication

Barnard, David T. (David Thomas), 1951–
   With skilful hand : the story of King David / David T. Barnard.
   (McGill-Queen's studies in the history of religion ; 29)
   Includes bibliographical references.
   ISBN 0-7735-2714-1
   1. David, King of Israel. I. Title. II. Series.
BS580.D3B37 2004   222'.4092   C2004-901109-X

Typeset in Palatino 10/13
by Caractéra inc., Quebec City

Contents

Preface   ix

Prologue   3

1 Preparation   6

2 Foundation   53

3 Reign   80

4 Dynasty   123

5 Reflection   138

Epilogue   162

APPENDICES

1 Names of People   167

2 Names of Places   179

3 Sources   183

4 The Contributors   185

5 Guide to Further Reading   190

Preface

The story told in this book is based on the text of the David stories in the Bible. Some of my favourite childhood memories are of learning these stories from my father, who would tell them with enthusiasm to my brothers and me at bedtime. I have tried to pass on some of that enthusiasm to my own children. Years ago one of them referred to the story commonly known as "David and Goliath" by the title "David and His Cousins Go Camping." This was a reference to the encampment of the army of Israel opposite the Philistines, and a confusion of David's brothers with his cousins. I realized that my own passion to interpret and apply might have misdirected attention from some of the key points of the stories.

In this book I attempt to interpret but to provide as well a faithful focus on the original stories. I take them as I find them in the Bible as a basis for my retelling, setting aside the interesting questions about sources, editorial intention, and so on. The material in Chronicles is straightforwardly merged with the stories in Samuel. I make the historically inaccurate assumption that literacy and access to writing materials were universal.

The idea of writing this form of book arose in a conversation with Don Akenson and Cathy Harland while travelling by train from Montreal to Kingston. I am grateful for their initial enthusiasm and subsequent advice. I received encouragement and advice along the way from Donna Achtzehner, George Baxter, Gail Bowen (whose persuasiveness and tact surpassed the claims of either collegiality or friendship), Ted Bowen, Saros Cowasjee, Maureen Garvie (McGill-Queen's University Press), David Kaiser, George Logan, Roger Martin, Rabbi Dow Marmur, Ken Mitchell, Eugene Peterson, Kathy Yanni, and readers assigned by McGill-Queen's University Press. My daughter, Stephanie, would not let me forget that I was not making progress on this project during a long period when indeed I was not! Benjamin and Rebecca have also participated in many discussions about these stories and this book.

While working on this project, I was able to visit a number of libraries to use material about David and his era. I am grateful to the institutions and to those persons who helped me at Bibliothèque de la Faculté Libre de Théologie Protestante, Paris; Bibliothèque Oecuménique et Scientifique pour l'Étude de la Bible (Bibliothèque Jean de Vernon), Institut Catholique de Paris; and Theology Faculty Library, Oxford University, Oxford. In Canada I owe special gratitiude to McMaster University Library, Hamilton; Regent College Library, Vancouver; Stauffer Library, Queen's University, Kingston; University of British Columbia Library, Vancouver; and University of Regina Library, Regina.

I had opportunities to use some of my material with classes in several churches. I thank those people who gave me advice at St Mark's Anglican Church, Versailles; Bay Park Baptist Church, Kingston; and First Baptist Church, Regina.

All of the poetry in this book, as well as any other material attributed to David in the first four sections, is taken verbatim from the Bible. In the story of David and Goliath I have used Ariella Deem's suggestion (see the guide to further reading in the appendix of this book) that the stone locked Goliath's greave and tripped him up rather than hitting him in the forehead.

If I had learned more from my father and these stories rather than in part – as King David did – from my own experience, I might have had a better book and had it sooner. My wife, Marcia, has supported me while I experienced and learned and wrote this book. With much gratitude for all of that, I dedicate this work to her.

WITH SKILFUL HAND

Then the Lord awoke as from sleep,
   like a warrior shouting because of wine.
He put his adversaries to rout;
   he put them to everlasting disgrace.

He rejected the tent of Joseph,
   he did not choose the tribe of Ephraim;
but he chose the tribe of Judah,
   Mount Zion, which he loves.
He built his sanctuary like the high heavens,
   like the earth, which he has founded forever.
He chose his servant David,
   and took him from the sheepfolds;
from tending the nursing ewes he brought him
   to be the shepherd of his people Jacob,
   of Israel, his inheritance.
With upright heart he tended them,
   and guided them with skilful hand.
                      Psalm 78: 65–72

Prologue

Zadok the Scribe Outlines His Project

It has been over six hundred years since David, son of Jesse, became king of Israel. He not only established a dynasty but also became an ideal. His fame is so great that all other kings of our nation since his reign have been measured against him. Our sacred books contain stories about him, and there are official records of his heroic acts and his establishment of a system of government and worship as well as other practices for our nation. These ancient texts are terse: they tell the stories, but they are focused on the king himself. They do not give much insight into the experiences of participants in those events. Even David's own motives and feelings are not always clear.

But there are other documents not included in the sacred texts.

In my youth, during the resettling and rebuilding of our nation when the people of Israel returned to our land following a period of captivity and deportation, I was given responsibility in the temple precincts. As worship and practices were being restored, I helped look after the storerooms where tithes, offerings, and temple articles were kept.

My first task was to clear away the accumulation built up from years of neglect and abuse. While doing so I came upon a bundle of documents. There was no time to deal with them then, given the urgency and importance of the work before us, so after reading enough to determine what they were, I put them aside in my own quarters. I have now had these documents for many years and have been greatly intrigued by them. In my late years I have realized that I should take responsibility for sorting, preserving, and presenting them to other readers.

It was a thrill for me to discover these documents and a privilege to work with them. The task of my last few years has been to put them in order, to decipher some of the more obscure parts, to interpret the various hands that wrote them, and to assemble this collection. More importantly for me, they have given me insight into a life that has always fascinated me.

Few stories are told in such detail in our sacred books as the story of David's life and his establishing of his dynasty. Yet few stories leave so many questions. Why did he do some of the things he did? How could God choose a man with such potential for grand failures? What general lessons should the faithful learn from these stories, and what is peculiar to the circumstances of this king's individual life?

There are no easy answers to these questions. It is clear from reading the history of our nation since David's reign that all other kings have been judged by his standard. And this judgment has not been simply that of the people, although they have certainly kept the ideal of David alive in their minds and conversation. It is also a judgment explicitly made by the servants of God who have chronicled the events.

Moses established our nation by leading us out of Egypt. David established the kingdom and the dynasty that has ruled it. God called both of them his servants and has not given that title to any other in our history. Moses built the Ark and used it as a focus for worship in the desert; David brought the Ark into the nation's new capital and used it as a focus for worship in the kingdom established in the promised land. God made a covenant with the people through Moses to be our God and to make us a nation; God made a covenant with the people through David to establish a dynasty of kings to be his regents among us.

These are the major themes of David's life, though many of the details seem difficult or ambiguous. The sacred stories and the various perspectives in these other documents that I have arranged here still do not tell all that one would like to know about this king.

The documents I found are brief, and many are personal. They are copies of letters written to friends or family members, and of personal journal entries, and fragments of formal records. They were kept together by someone who was part of, or close to, those events. Perhaps they were gathered and preserved by King David's seer and friend, the musician Heman. He would certainly have been in a position to record David's remarks made late in life. But whatever hand collected them, it left no explicit trace – no reason, no signature, no authority, no comments.

I have arranged the documents in chronological order based on the events to which they refer. In most cases this is also the order in which I believe them to have been written, but where that is not the case, I have made a note to that effect.

My study of these documents, together with the ancient texts passed down to us, confirms my belief that they were gathered to enrich the story. They set out the hopes, the aspirations, and the frustrations of many who participated in the well-known stories about King David. Few documents are from David's own hand; to make up for this lack, I have included some of his songs taken from our sacred texts written on occasions that prompted other writers to balance their reflections with those of David.

I have organized the collection into five parts. The first four correspond to several stages in David's life and career: preparation for rule, the founding of the kingdom, his reign, and the establishment of his dynasty. The fifth part is notes from a series of addresses given by David in old age to the company of singers he had assembled to participate in worship. My organization of the first four parts follows the flow of David's thought in these addresses.

I do not know why these documents were not included in the sacred texts. Perhaps the collector did not wish them to be seen because they reveal the humanness of David and those close to him. Sometimes it is not good to diminish a hero. Perhaps the editors of the sacred books themselves rejected these documents. In any case, it is a loss not to have them, so I make them available here.

The story of David has long fascinated me. If I am honest, I must admit I have taken longer to prepare these documents than was necessary. The delay results from my own uncertainty. I wanted to find here an explanation for David's actions, some of which are strange to me. But I have found that even those close to David often did not fully understand him. I wanted to gain assurance, as David claims to have had, that a life devoted to God – complete with errors made and sins committed – is the life worth living. I am an old man, alone since my wife has gone to our ancestors and my daughter has decided to keep to herself in Jericho. I have lived as a religious man, immersed in ancient texts and rituals. I have never experienced God speaking to me as he spoke to some in these stories. I wanted to be assured that my choice to serve the God of our ancestors – the God of David – has been worthwhile.

1 Preparation

Zadok the Scribe's Commentary

The stories about David begin when he was a young man in his father's home and then in the service of King Saul. The God of our ancestors was displeased with Saul and intended to replace him as king of Israel. David needed time to develop and refine the qualities God wanted in a king, some of which had begun to appear while he was on his father's farm. But long before Saul's reign ended, David was identified as the next king – first secretly by God and then in a growing expectation among the people. This was a time of tension in the nation and in the lives of those around both men. The first group of documents is from that early period before David became king.

David's father, Jesse, and his mother, Jannah, lived at Bethlehem. Some of the earliest documents are family correspondence, especially with nearby friends.

As David was drawn into the life of the court, some of Saul's family (son Jonathan and daughter Michal, who both loved David) and officials (General Abner, the shepherd Doeg) began to write about David. Other insights have been provided by servants of God: priests Ahimelech and Abiathar, the prophet Samuel. This latter group was in danger from Saul because their allegiance was ultimately not to the king but to God – and they several times felt themselves called by God to do or say things that would anger the king. Saul turned against David, who was repeatedly forced to flee, even to the extent of taking refuge with Israel's traditional enemies, the Philistines.

As David built his own life and relationships, there were letters from some of his wives and his own family members. The wives were

Abigail, whom he met in the desert, Ahinoam, the mother of his first-born son, and Michal, Saul's daughter. David's sister Zeruiah had three sons – Joab, Abishai, and Asahel – who were leaders among David's warriors when he developed his own following. They were valuable in their roles but at the same time a source of trouble to him throughout his life. Their family correspondence provides several revealing insights into their lives.

Our nation of Israel was still being formed in David's time. King Saul was the first king of the nation formed from knitting together the twelve tribes descended from the patriarch Israel. But individual tribal identities were still important, especially for some of the dominant tribes. David was from Judah, one such tribe. The early stages of his life often reflect a struggle between these two identities: the tribal identity in Judah and the national identity in Israel.

Some of the most dramatic stories of David's career come from this period. But it is also a difficult period of David's life to understand. A good few of these documents show the complications of life for those close to him during these ambiguous early days before he came to power. But even for those close to him, it becomes clear that much of what David did and said was not well understood either by his enemies or by those who supported and loved him. He was a difficult man to know even for those who lived with him, and that difficulty has only increased in the years since his death.

1.01 Samuel Anoints David
Eliab, David's brother (at Bethlehem), writes to his friend, Ashhur (at Tekoa)

Ash,

The next time your family passes through on the way to Jerusalem, you must convince your father to stop. You and I have complained so often that nothing happens out here in these small towns, but now something has. We have had a visit from Samuel, the prophet! That's something I never expected in this boring place. And I'm not the only one – his coming surprised everyone, especially my father.

It's very strange, and worth some talk when I see you. The prophet came to our town and met with the elders. Not that he sought them out – they went to him on the road, the old fools, worried about why he had come. They feared he might have been angry with them or at the community, for something said or not said, done or not done – you know how it can be with them when they get started. But it's understandable to be like that with Samuel – he's that way himself. We have heard stories about him before, and some of the things that provoke him seem so petty.

He told the elders he had only come to make a sacrifice. He invited them, especially naming my father – saying, "I want to see that faithful Judahite, Jesse" – to sacrifice with him. My father couldn't understand it, especially when Samuel asked him to bring his sons as well. At my father's age, many things easily upset him.

The ceremony was a welcome change from the emptiness of our regular services. Old Samuel has a reputation for becoming easily angered and says that much of what he sees around him does not please God. He talks about God as though about another person. And those prayers we have repeated so often and complained about so much, he makes them seem as if they are words actually spoken *to* somebody.

After the ceremony he sat with the council and talked. My father sat next to him. The others forced him to, saying Samuel had mentioned him by name, but really nobody else was comfortable sitting there. After a while the two of them called me over. I didn't know why: Samuel looked as though he wanted to talk to me as I approached, but when I got there he just greeted me and said a blessing, and I was sent away. He then did the same with each of the others in my family. A greeting, a blessing, a dismissal.

Why us, why our family? We aren't the most important in Bethlehem or the richest. And as for keeping the faith, well … I know Samuel called my father faithful – it's being repeated everywhere around town – but my father sometimes treats his own sacrifices as wasteful extravagances he grudges giving. How did Samuel even know about us?

He wasn't just content with seeing those of us who were there. He asked if there were any others. When he heard about David, he had my father send for him. My father had left him looking after the sheep while we prepared for the sacrifice rather than bother sending someone to relieve him. But the prophet wanted to meet all of us, and the old man's wishes are indulged in this country.

People would rather do what Samuel asks than have him angry and claiming God's support for his anger.

When David came, Samuel seemed at last to take some interest. He and my father and David sat apart from us and spoke together. Then they called the family together, and Samuel anointed David. What can that mean, Ash? Perhaps the child told some of his stories or sang some of his silly songs! He can't even seem to take the farm work seriously, and he's useless to the family except when he's in the fields with the sheep. Whatever the reason, none of them spoke of it afterward or of what was said among them.

My father gets agitated when I ask about it, and David himself, in his aggravating way, won't say anything. He's back to the fields now and good riddance.

So now I have seen Samuel, Ash, the one of whom the stories speak. He is real, and the world outside this ridiculous village of Bethlehem is real, and I want to get out there and see it. I know some of my brothers feel the same way. I know you want something more out of life too. If I'm to have a chance at life elsewhere it must be soon, before my father dies saddling me with the responsibility for the farm. When you visit, we can talk.

Eliab

1.02 Samuel Is Surprised by God
Samuel (at Bethlehem) writes to Gad the Prophet (at Ramah)

My dear young colleague,
Blessed be God, protector of his people, who has again kept me safe. When he sent me to Bethlehem to anoint one of the sons of Jesse of Bethlehem as the next king, I was afraid. Saul is a dangerous man, willing to use his power to punish those who obstruct him. I know he has become suspicious of everything I do since I told him that the God of our ancestors has determined to replace him as king.

The trip to Bethlehem took place without any difficulty from King Saul. The sacrifice we made there, my students and I, together with the local council, will surely seem to him sufficient cause for the visit when it is reported to him, as I know it will be.

So this mission came off without complications, but not without surprises. Even after all these years, God can still surprise me. And the people of the land think that I am the one who is difficult to understand! I made a point of seeing Jesse of Bethlehem, as I had understood from the oracle, and asking for his sons. When I saw the first-born I rejoiced – he is handsome, strong, and confident of himself. He is the kind of man people want to follow, and I thought God had sent me to anoint him.

You have asked me how you can know that God is speaking to you. I must confess that sometimes I still find it difficult. As a young boy when I first heard God speak to me, I mistook what I heard for the voice of my teacher. But eventually I learned to know God's voice, just as you will. This is what I have already taught you; it is an oracle. We hear the actual words of God. Sometimes, though, the oracle is not explicit and complete. That is what happened to me with respect to Jesse's first-born. I had a clear word from God to anoint a son of Jesse in Bethlehem. I assumed it would be the first-born, and my impression of him was positive.

But this was not to be. As I stood there, God spoke to me in the quiet of my inner being, to tell me that he considers what a person *is* – the heart – rather than how he looks. This is another way that God speaks to me and to all of us prophets. Sometimes we have the ecstatic response of almost being carried along by the words that come from God so that we can do nothing else but speak them as quickly as we understand them. And sometimes the word of God comes in quietness, requiring careful listening and sensitive reflection. You will experience God in this way yourself, I predict, because you are receptive to God and to those around you.

Of course I knew that God considers the heart, not the physical appearance, but I thought he would at least pick a king who is visibly a leader. Certainly when he chose Saul, the people immediately responded to the choice, and now I expected – I wanted – another such choice.

Instead, I had to see all the sons of Jesse without finding the man God had appointed for me to meet. The word had been so sure – "Bethlehem, one of the sons of Jesse" – that I could not have mistaken it. So I questioned Jesse further and found there was another son, the youngest, out with the sheep, not invited to the sacrifice. I had Jesse bring him, and he was the one.

Not what I expected. Just a boy, really. An attractive youth, but years from being the leader of the people of God. It was a disappointment to me. I am ready for this period of uncertainty with Saul to end.

Nonetheless, God was in it. When I touched the forehead of this boy (his name is David) with the oil on my fingers, I could tell that the spirit of God came to him. The spirit did not come in ecstasy, but it came. The boy will need to learn how to live with that!

I need to think about this. I will have Saul for a long time yet, and I find that difficult already – as does Saul himself. I've been surprised by God yet again. I'm too old for surprises.

In haste,
Samuel

1.03 David Protects the Sheep
Jannah (at Bethlehem) writes to her friend Miriam (at Tekoa)

My dear friend,
Jesse has said that he will join your husband on business to Jerusalem for two days next week. Could you come this far and stay with me overnight? It has been so long since we have had time to speak to each other.

If Ashhur can be spared from the work, bring him. Eliab would enjoy a chance to visit with him, so the two could act for Jesse in looking after our farm. They would get a taste of the larger responsibilities they seem to want so much. Perhaps they will see that the responsibilities they think so attractive are not so easy to carry. I worry about Eliab and his eagerness for something new and different from the life on the farm.

If you come, though, as I hope you will, I really want to talk not about my eldest son but about my youngest. David is growing up so quickly, changing as all boys do, but sometimes in ways almost not recognizable to me. He came home from the sheep a week ago with a story of how a bear had attacked the flock and how he had taken a sheep back from the bear and then killed the bear with his hands. There was a similar story about a lion, of all things, earlier this year. His brothers were sceptical, but searching the fields on both occasions, they saw the bodies of the animals and claim there were no marks from weapons on them.

Twice now David seems to have been fortunate – protected by God, he says, and who's to argue with that? But what would make him want to do this, to fight an animal, especially without weapons? When he is taunted by those who don't believe him, he insists even more that God has enabled him to accomplish these feats. Have I given birth to a fool?

You see? I worry. I miss talking with you. Will you come?

With affection,
Jannah

1.04 David Goes to the Court of Saul
Jesse (at Bethlehem) writes to his friend Eliab (at Tekoa)

Eliab, my old friend,
My life is becoming complicated at a time when I would have it simpler. My eldest, named for you but so unlike you, wants "excitement" that he cannot find here in Bethlehem, and is making me miserable with his discontent. My youngest, David, has gone to court at the king's request.

This was as unexpected to me as that visit from Samuel two years ago. For a long time I thought that David would be content to be a shepherd (he seems to enjoy the solitude), but he may not be given the chance. Today another messenger has come from the king, asking that David be allowed to remain in his service as an armour bearer. I questioned the messenger closely to know what the king wants with my son. He told me that David was summoned, and has now been asked to stay, because some courtier passing through Bethlehem heard him play his harp in the market. It seems that his music soothes the king.

How can I refuse, even though I would rather have him here?

Does a family ever develop the way a father expects it to, Eliab?

So, I send you my apologies that I was not able to come to the road to see you on your return from the north this time. Shammah, who brings you this message, also brings a piece of the sheep we roasted for our meal with the king's messenger today. Send word the next time you will pass by Bethlehem.

Jesse

1.05 David and Goliath
Eliab, David's brother (at Elah), writes to his friend Ashhur (at Tekoa)

Ash,
Perhaps you chose better than I, staying in your father's shop. At least one day you will inherit a respectable business (I hear it may be soon; how is your father's health?) while my hopes for success in this army may come to nothing. My brothers Abinadab and Shammah are also wondering if this choice was a good one.

King Saul has had so many victories in the past that all of us who joined up for this campaign against the Philistines were expecting victory again. And with victory we expected feasts, Philistine women, some share of the spoils. I was hoping that my share would be enough for me to start life somewhere other than Bethlehem.

But Saul found no victory this time. We were in a humiliating, frustrating position for weeks, camped opposite the Philistines here – they on one side of the valley, we on the other. They proposed a battle of champions. Their champion was like something out of childhood bedtime tales – huge, almost inhuman, this Goliath from the stronghold at Gath, standing half again as tall as a normal man. No one in this army, not even among the leaders or the veterans, could stand a chance against him. The king searched the ranks for someone to respond for us, even offering wealth and marriage to his daughter as inducements, but no one was foolish enough to volunteer.

I expect you know this much already – who in this entire nation does not? We are close enough to home that this embarrassment must be the talk in every marketplace. But the latest thing is news indeed, as it just happened yesterday. Good for Israel, I suppose, and for the army, but terrible for me.

My father wanted to know for himself what was happening to the host, so sent David with a gift to my commander and some food for me and my brothers. I had thought that at least here we were well clear of him! Sadly not. When the boy heard the Philistine's challenge, he asked, in that falsely naive manner of his, why no warrior of the host of God would stand against this unbeliever, and what reward there would be for the man who fought for Israel. I tried to shut him up, but he kept on about it so much that the king heard about the commotion and sent for him.

You can imagine what this was like, Ash. He is not much more than a child, but there he was talking to the king with many of the soldiers looking on and listening. I tried to stay close but out of sight. He asked his questions again, still in that innocent way he has. He seemed to think fighting Goliath was no great thing – because God is with us, he said. Saul was so desperate for a champion that he agreed to have even David! They tried to dress him as a soldier from Saul's own equipment stores but the boy could not manage the armour.

So he went unarmed except for his sling, some stones he picked up from the ground, and his staff – a shepherd youth going to fight a warrior. Except for Saul's involvement, the entire thing would have been a joke. It certainly seemed like one to Goliath, who became even more obnoxious once he saw we were sending a boy against him. He and David yelled back and forth as they got closer, with David repeating his nonsense about God protecting Israel and defeating the Philistines. At least the boy can run – our chasing has taught him that! So he ran at Goliath and slung a stone. What luck the boy has, Ash! The stone stuck in the giant's knee greave so that he could not walk. As he tripped and fell, David was quickly beside him and grabbed Goliath's own sword to behead him.

The next hours were glorious. The Philistines were shocked and totally unprepared for battle when we quickly came at them. We chased them back to their own cities, killing many along the way. I myself got one of them and have his armband to prove it. Then we returned to take the spoils from their camp.

Of course the king and the entire army wanted to know who this giant killer was. Now everyone knows he is David ben-Jesse of Bethlehem. Everyone also knows he is my brother. It's bad to be in an army held at bay by a single person as we've been by Goliath. We will be mocked for it when we return home. Here the others are taking out their own frustrations by continually asking how my younger brother, just a shepherd, became a better and braver soldier than I. It has not been fun.

As I said, maybe staying at home would have been a better choice. At least I'll get some advantage from this, and have the boy carry this letter to you on his way home. When the host is dismissed (perhaps shortly, as there will be little threat from the lords of the Philistines for a while now) I will return to Bethlehem and surely visit you in Tekoa soon after.

Eliab

1.06 A Boy to Watch
Abner, Saul's general (at Elah) writes to his father, Ner (at Jericho)

Dear Father,
The standoff against the Philistine army and its champion, Goliath, ended today. Goliath was bested in personal combat by David ben-Jesse of Bethlehem, acting on behalf of the army of Israel. This David is not a member of the army but was apparently visiting some brothers of his when he heard the challenge. David had no armour. The fight between them was short. They exchanged words, David launched one stone from his shepherd's sling that tripped up the giant, then used Goliath's own sword to behead him.

With Goliath dead, I immediately led the army across the valley to attack the Philistine position. They were unprepared and ran before us. We chased them back to the coast, almost to the gates of their strongholds in Gath and Ekron. They suffered many casualties in the rout while we lost only a few.

We took the spoils from their camp when we returned. The king made a special gift of Goliath's weapons to David. David also took the giant's head with him – even carrying it in his interview with Saul after the battle! That was one of the strangest parts of the entire experience. He seemed to believe it was expected of him to do so, a necessary sign that he had accomplished the task. He was almost embarrassed by it, perhaps aware that it was a grisly thing. And yet for brief moments he also seemed to flaunt that head and to revel in the attention, as if some childish bravado carried him on.

The king is heartened by the victory but did not enter the battle himself. It is good that this season is almost over and that he will have time to recover his will before we must face these coast-dwellers again.

This David ben-Jesse bears watching. I have not often seen such fearlessness. He claims to have done this deed to honour God, but surely the prospect of what the king was offering – a reward and the hand of his daughter, Merab, in marriage – must have been in the boy's mind as well. Perhaps better to risk life for those rewards than to face his lot as the youngest son in a farmer's large family. That would certainly have been some inducement for me! But if he thought about it, he did not mention it to Saul. And Saul will doubtless not mention the rewards again unless they are asked for! I wonder if the boy has the nerve to claim them.

My cousin Saul was today overshadowed by a mere boy. He will not like that.

With love,
Abner

1.07 David and Jonathan Find a New Friendship
Jonathan, Saul's son (at Elah) writes to his uncle, Ner (at Jericho)

Dear Uncle,
Today my father's disgrace at the hand of the Philistines ended. A young man of Bethlehem, David ben-Jesse, fought this Goliath we have all feared so much, and defeated him easily! I wish now that I had shown the courage he showed, and I have heard many others say the same thing. Some, of course, want to make it a small thing – anyone could have done it, they say. But he is the one who did it!

When he stood before my father with Goliath's head in his hand, I was drawn to him and his sincerity. In the midst of this war camp he speaks in such a natural way of God and God's presence with the nation and with him. He does not swagger and boast beyond his actions as so many of my father's soldiers and generals do. They have been particularly irritating during this period of inactivity forced on us by Goliath's unmet challenge. Surely David will go with us now. My father will not let such a valuable servant be wasted on a farm!

I gave him my royal robes and my personal weapons to show my love for him. It will be good to have him in the household. I have found being the king's son a burden hard to bear, impossible to share. But this David seems so different, so sure of himself. I would like to have that self-assurance. I know you have often spoken to me about this, but I do not want the public life of a king.

With respect,
Jonathan

1.08 Saul Is Jealous of David
Abner, Saul's general (at Gibeah) writes to his father, Ner (at Jericho)

Dearest Father,
Can I continue to hold in balance these forces at work all around me?

At first King Saul was pleased whenever David ben-Jesse succeeded in some errand or mission. But now the king's jealousy makes him unpredictable. That foolish song the people are singing – about enemies conquered, giving David the credit for tens of thousands of enemies killed and Saul the credit for only thousands – is like a goad to him.

He has tried twice to kill David with his own spear. David regularly plays his harp in the court to please and calm the king. But sometimes the presence of David is more a provocation than the music is a release. And on those occasions Saul doesn't relax, he gets angry. It's unpredictable. But twice while David has played, Saul has grabbed his spear and attempted to impale David. The first time he was so angry that he threw it wildly. This second time the courtiers were more alert and called out a warning before the spear was thrown.

How would we have explained David's death to Jesse and to the people? Even Jonathan, as much as he accepts his father's moods, would not have let that pass!

Now David has been sent to lead his thousand against the Philistines. I believe that Saul, knowing how daring David can be, hopes that the young man will be killed. But though Saul is a successful fighter himself, he cannot see that David's wit balances his daring, so that he seldom fights when he cannot win.

I suspect David knows the king's hope too but that he is pleased to be away from the court and out where it is at least clear who is the enemy! He managed to evade Saul's offer of Merab as wife before he left, so Saul has now consented to Merab's desire to marry another man. Perhaps David knew that such a marriage would have kept him dangerously close to Saul.

These intrigues are distasteful to me. I didn't expect this when I agreed to serve with Saul. He should keep his attention on the affairs of the nation.

Love,
Abner

1.09 Michal Loves David
Michal (at Gibeah) writes to her cousin Marah (at Jericho)

Cousin,
You must come quickly. I am to marry, and I want you to help me prepare and celebrate.

You will have heard the stories and songs about my father's general, David ben-Jesse. I've not told you before, but I have loved him for years. I can't recall when he first came to court. I think it was after one of the Philistine wars – no, perhaps it was before that, the winter before, when he came to serve my father as court musician. Whenever it was, at first I did not find him attractive. He looked and dressed like a poor farmer. And he seemed so young! That was in part, I think, because he had spent so much time with his father's sheep and so little time with other people that he was very naive.

He was so uncouth when he came to court! He didn't know how to eat at the king's table, how to behave with the king or his court, how to handle weapons and war. He was awkward and embarrassing. The only thing he could do with any grace was make music. He played the harp and wrote wonderful songs that soothed my father. He became a close friend to my brother, but I wanted nothing to do with him.

Gradually, though, I came to love him. Because he was often in the king's presence to play his music I could not avoid seeing him. He quickly took up the pattern and manners of the court. He was always friendly to everyone, but somehow distant – as though he was thinking about other things than the details of life around him.

Perhaps that is why his songs are so intriguing and soothing. He seems to take my father and other listeners to some distant place that fades away when he stops singing.

He has grown to be strong and impressively at ease with my father and the other warriors and generals. His physical presence is exciting. The men in his thousand talk about him and his battle skill whenever they are here in Gibeah. He is a hero to them. It's his passion, I think – when he fights he fights with skill and daring. He seems to have no fear, they say. And the results are beyond what any other general achieves. You know that the people sing in the streets when he returns from battle.

The passion he uses in war is evident in other aspects of his life. He's devoted himself to learning the ways of the court. He has learned manners and grace; he's learned to speak well. The passion is also evident in his devotion to God, to whom he gives credit for all he does. He is so full of emotion and energy. He seems to run at life and grab it to be lived and experienced. He is not particularly handsome, so don't expect him to be the kind of man we always told each other we wanted, but there's an attractiveness that comes from his energy – perhaps I should say his spirit.

When he returns from battle, everyone crowds around to hear the stories. When first they are told by the men of his troop (his thousand), they make David the hero. And then David takes a turn, making his men the heroes and God the cause of victory. Most of my father's generals are full of themselves and their exploits. They make themselves out to be more than they are. But David has no apparent desire to do that. I worry when he is away and rejoice when he returns safely. Then I join the others to hear the stories, and long to be the one to whom he will reveal his private thoughts.

Things are difficult between David and my father. I think the king values him and at the same time fears him. David should have had my sister Merab as wife years ago as a reward for some battle deed, but he claimed he could not accept such an honour. That would have been hard for me to bear! Instead of marrying my sister, he has been away as captain of one of my father's thousands, and has returned with stories of success that almost require the king to honour him again.

Though women in Israel do not often talk of love for men, I have spoken to my sister about my love for David, and she has told the king. My father, knowing I love David, offered again that David become his son-in-law, and this time David has accepted. I'm embarrassed by the bride price. My father asked for a hundred Philistine foreskins, meaning, I'm sure, to let David demonstrate his battle skills again (though some say my father wanted to put him in danger again). But David took him literally, and with his men got twice the number – two hundred bits of flesh that he brought in a basket before the king! I would rather have had another price, but it's paid now. My father must have been embarrassed too, because he seemed very agitated when David brought in his bloody basket. (Or so I'm told – I wasn't there.)

Both of them are anxious to have the marriage concluded. We have set a day next week, so you must come quickly to help me. My father has given us a house where we can live close by the court. You must visit us there too, but not immediately after the marriage! My mother will make you welcome for a few days here until you return home. The messenger who brings this will escort you if you are able to come.

Michal

1.10 David in Danger from Saul
Jonathan, Saul's son (at Gibeah), writes to his uncle Ner (at Jericho)

Dear Uncle,
The situation between David and my father has totally deteriorated. Last month my father, wanting to kill David, told those of us close to him to look for an opportunity. I hid David and defended him in conversation with my father. Since then things have grown worse.

The king briefly relented, because he knows in his heart that David means him no harm, but he was provoked again by jealousy over David's latest victories over the Philistines. I had thought it a good thing when David went out to battle this last time, a chance for my father to cool down. But it's had just the opposite effect.

In his throne room this afternoon my father again tried to kill David with a spear. Several of the generals were back from raids. They were boasting of their exploits as they do, each trying to convince my father that he is the most skilful and most devoted.

David was part of the cheering as each spoke. When his own turn came and he described his latest victories, it was clear that he and his thousand had done more damage to our enemies than any of the others. We all knew that this was a dangerous time, because my father's reactions to David's victories are unpredictable. The king became angry and grabbed his spear, and threw it. But several were watching him and cried out, and David ran from the room.

The king resents all that David has accomplished. When he came to us, David was only a farm boy, a shepherd. Now the people consider him a champion. His exploits surpass those of the king himself. My father, I think, has never been entirely comfortable with the kingship, and he is threatened by David and public recognition of David's success. Worse, it is clear to him that David is a favourite among those who serve God, and this worries him.

David has fled, presumably to his own home, but some of the king's own guard are missing from the court this evening. I am afraid they may have gone to hunt for David. I don't know if I can dissuade my father this time. He was as distressed today as he has ever been. David's music did not soothe him. Anything about David now provokes an irrational response from him. I am afraid for David tonight.

I pray that God, if he listens to princes, will hear me now and protect my father from his foolishness and my friend from this danger. Does God listen to princes, uncle?

With respect,
Jonathan

1.11 Michal Is Separated from David
Michal (at Gibeah) writes to her cousin, Marah (at Jericho)

Cousin,
It would be a great comfort if you could come to be with me for a few days. The strife between my father and my husband has become so extreme that the king has tried repeatedly to kill David. Now David has fled with his thousand, and the king's army is in pursuit.

About a week ago David returned from countering another attack by the Philistines moving in from the coast against our farming lands. I have been so proud of him in his exploits – all the people talk and sing about what he does in battle. But this has only angered my father again. I tell you, cousin, sometimes I don't recognize him when this anger comes upon him.

After the battle report my father tried to kill David again, but he ran from the court and came to me at the house. While we were talking about what we would do, we heard sounds in the street. David looked out and saw some men watching the house. He recognized them as part of the palace guard.

I knew he would be taken in the morning, and I feared he would never escape again. I had to let him out a window into a neighbouring courtyard in the night, and he has gone away. When the men came for him I stalled them, filling the bed to look as though he lay there and saying he was ill. When they came a second time at my father's order, they were prepared to carry him out in his bed!

My father is very angry about my helping David escape. David cannot return to me. Apparently he cannot even send me word, because I have had no message telling me where he is! And I am afraid of my father now.

Marriage to my father's champion has been much less than what I expected it to be. David does not return my love with equal passion. He is more concerned with his battles and his men than with me. I'm often alone because he is away on raids. And now this! I don't know if he will be able to return soon – or ever!

My father was angrier today than ever before. He cares nothing for me, it seems. I was given to David not because I wanted that union but apparently to keep David close to my father. And what David wants I cannot know.

I'm alone and afraid. Would you come for a day or two? I long for your company.

In need again,
Michal

1.12 David's Meditation: Saul Watches His House
David writes at Gibeah

> Deliver me from my enemies, O my God;
>   protect me from those who rise up against me.
> Deliver me from those who work evil;
>   from the bloodthirsty save me.

Even now they lie in wait for my life;
> the mighty stir up strife against me.
For no transgression or sin of mine, O Lord,
> for no fault of mine, they run and make ready.

Rouse yourself, come to my help and see!
> You, Lord God of hosts, are God of Israel.
Awake to punish all the nations;
> spare none of those who treacherously plot evil.

Each evening they come back,
> howling like dogs
> and prowling about the city.
There they are, bellowing with their mouths,
> with sharp words on their lips –
> for "Who," they think, "will hear us?"

But you laugh at them, O Lord;
> you hold all the nations in derision.
O my strength, I will watch for you;
> for you, O God, are my fortress.
My God in his steadfast love will meet me;
> my God will let me look in triumph on my enemies.

Do not kill them, or my people may forget;
> make them totter by your power, and bring them down,
> O Lord, our shield.
For the sin of their mouths, the words of their lips,
> let them be trapped in their pride.
For the cursing and lies that they utter,
> consume them in wrath;
> consume them until they are no more.
Then it will be known to the ends of the earth
> that God rules over Jacob.

Each evening they come back,
> howling like dogs
> and prowling about the city.
They roam about for food,
> and growl if they do not get their fill.

But I will sing of your might;
  I will sing aloud of your steadfast love in the morning.
For you have been a fortress for me
  and a refuge in the day of my distress.
O my strength, I will sing praises to you,
  for you, O God, are my fortress,
  the God who shows me steadfast love.

1.13 Samuel Fears Saul's Wrath
Samuel the prophet (at Ramah) writes to Gad the prophet (at Jericho)

Dear young colleague,
Blessed be God, the All Wise, whose ways are beyond human understanding.

David ben-Jesse came to me today with the story of how King Saul has again tried to kill him. David has escaped with the help of his wife, Michal. I cannot understand why God does not act to remove Saul and let David assume the kingship for which I anointed him years ago.

I took David to the school of the prophets so that he could seek the face of God and the wisdom of God. But before we could discern anything, men came from Saul to seek him. The ecstasy came upon them, though, and they prophesied instead of carrying out Saul's orders. He sent a second band of men, and the same thing happened. So he sent a third band, and it happened a third time.

Finally the king came himself. But the ecstasy even came upon him! By the time he joined us, he was overcome, and he lay before me to speak his oracle, as the others had done earlier. While I was occupied with the king, David fled. I do not know where he has gone. I fear for him. I fear for Saul. I fear for the people of Israel while the king fights his most successful general. What good can come of this? What is the will of God in this?

I hope that you can return quickly to me here. Give my greetings to our brothers at Jericho, but come now. I need to discuss all of this with you. We need to make plans to protect priests and prophets if there is a time of conflict coming between David and Saul.

In haste,
Samuel

1.14 Jonathan Protects David
Jonathan, Saul's son (at Gibeah), writes to his uncle Ner (at Jericho)

Dear Uncle,

I have sent my friend away from the court for his own protection, with the blessing of peace from God upon him. I pray that he may find it. Does God listen to princes, uncle?

David came to me while my father was still prophesying at the school of the prophets. What in the name of the All Powerful was that about? Saul is king. Is Saul among the prophets? David was convinced that the king wanted to kill him. He believed my father had come to the school of the prophets to do that and would have done so except for the ecstasy upon him.

I did not want to believe that of my father. Yet when I put him to a test the next day, it was obvious to me that David was right. David stayed away from the court, even though Saul expected him to be there. And I gave the excuse David suggested to me, that he had gone to Bethlehem to be with his family for a celebration there. My father's anger – at David, at me, even at my mother for bearing me – was beyond reason. I've never heard such a string of oaths from him before. When he threw his wine goblet, most at the table were ready to run. Fortunately that rash gesture seemed to use up the worst of his rage.

He wants David to die so that the kingdom will be assured for me. He cannot – will not – see that it's too late for that. The kingdom has passed from our family, as Samuel said years ago. I do not want it, even if it could be had. The pain it has caused to my father is more than I want to bear – to be king when the people do not want me.

I spoke to David at his hiding place in the fields this morning, covering up our meeting with archery practice so that my father and his guard would not see us. The future is uncertain now. Indeed, the future is always in the hands of the Lord, and we only delude ourselves into thinking we control it. In any case I recognize that it surely is in his hands now. Yet I still fear for my father and for my friend.

It gives me some comfort to communicate these matters to you. I miss the times when you used to visit. I wish you were well enough to come to us now. Your wisdom would be welcomed here – by me, certainly by Abner, and probably still even by my father.

He does not seem these days to have counsellors he can, or should, trust.

With respect,
Jonathan

1.15 David Finds Provisions
Ahimelech the priest (at Nob) writes to Samuel the prophet (at Ramah)

Wise one,
Blessed be the Lord, giver of light and understanding.

I am troubled tonight, my friend, by the strange events of the day. David ben-Jesse, the king's general, came to me with a handful of men on an undisclosed mission. Whatever his business, he had left the court in haste – without food or weapons!

What business of such urgency can there be in the kingdom? We have heard here of David's recent battles against the Philistines, but the reports we received told us that the Philistines were being forced back to the coastal plains again. Is there danger of another invasion? How much can the people of the Lord bear?

Or could there be trouble between David and Saul? You have told me how years ago you secretly anointed David to be king and how the Lord rejected Saul. And it is common knowledge that the king cannot control his jealousy of David. But if there is now conflict between them, why did David not speak of it? Does he trust no one?

David also was without weapons, which is surely strange for one of the king's most important generals. He asked me for a sword or spear. I had only the sword of Goliath, left here where we keep the ancient priestly garments after David's slaying of the giant some years ago. He took that. It is an amazing weapon that few could handle. Some of his men had weapons, but it is still a lightly armed party if they are to do battle.

I had no food to offer – we do not expect guests here, only worshippers – but there was some consecrated bread. The general told me his men were ceremonially clean, so I gave it to them. It seemed right to David and to me, old friend, to meet the needs of these servants of the king – and the Lord – with the bread consecrated to the Lord's presence. I hope that you can support my decision in this matter.

It was a busy day here. The king's chief shepherd, Doeg, arrived just after the troops left. He may be competent in his work, but I wish the king could have found another person for that role. He comes close to mocking the sacred rites, and I do not trust him.

I pray that the Keeper of Israel will be with David and his men to bless them in whatever they do in the king's name. I long for an understanding of the significance of all this. Send word to me when you learn what is happening. In the meantime, I hope that your student Gad is as much support to you in your lonely work as my son Abiathar is to me in mine.

Sincerely,
Ahimelech

1.16 David's Meditation: The Treachery of Doeg
David writes in the desert

> Why do you boast, O mighty one,
>   of mischief done against the godly?
>   All day long you are plotting destruction.
> Your tongue is like a sharp razor,
>   you worker of treachery.
> You love evil more than good,
>   and lying more than speaking the truth.
> You love all words that devour,
>   O deceitful tongue.
>
> But God will break you down forever;
>   he will snatch and tear you from your tent;
>   he will uproot you from the land of the living.
> The righteous will see, and fear,
>   and will laugh at the evildoer, saying,
> "See the one who would not take
>   refuge in God,
> but trusted in abundant riches,
>   and sought refuge in wealth!"

But I am like a green olive tree
>in the house of God.
I trust in the steadfast love of God
>forever and ever.
I will thank you forever,
>because of what you have done.
In the presence of the faithful
>I will proclaim your name, for it is good.

1.17 David Finds Shelter with the Philistines
Ira, annalist in the court of Achish (at Gath), writes in his journal

My lord Achish fares well in his battles against the cursed Israelites who block the expansion of our people to the east. Other Philistine lords are neither so skilful in battle nor so respected by our enemies. Earlier this year in battle with the Israelite commander David ben-Jesse, they were driven out of the Israelite lands.

But now there is trouble in Israel, and David ben-Jesse has quarrelled with their king, Saul. For some time we have had reports from our informants at that court about problems between these two. It appears that the alliance between them was not a strong one but simply a mercenary relationship. They share neither a sense of what their kingdom should be nor a commitment to the good of Saul's home tribe of Benjamin. With the quarrel now growing stronger, ben-Jesse has left Saul and come to the court of my lord Achish.

The band that ben-Jesse commands is famous for its battle prowess and doubtless would be of value to my lord. But ben-Jesse himself is a complex man, not easily known, not trusting, and doubtless not to be trusted. The people of Israel sing of him as a slayer of ten thousands, most of them Philistines and one of them our own great warrior Goliath.

My lord's councillors advised him against hiring this man and his men, useful though they may be. While the council met, ben-Jesse entered the chamber, apparently insane, scratching at the walls, making a nuisance of himself. This evidence of his instability convinced my lord Achish to abandon his plan to hire these men. They will now be treated as enemy soldiers, and their fate will be determined when the council sits again tomorrow.

1.18 David Hides Himself and His Family
Jesse (at Mizpah) writes to his friend Eliab (at Tekoa)

Eliab,
The world is changing and I do not like it. My son David has brought me and Jannah here – for safety, he says, from the king! One of my grandmothers came from this foreign place, you will have heard. It was certainly still talked about when we were children, though I myself never mention it. But no one from our family has been back here since then – or so I thought! David seems to have been everywhere in his fighting for Israel, and to know and be known by the commanders of the nations around us, and sometimes by the kings.

I had hoped when he married Michal that the troubles between him and the king would end, and that I would have grandchildren from him as from my other children. But my son and Saul still quarrel, and the king truly wants to kill him. David has told us this before, but I would not believe it then. He left his wife behind and went with some of his soldiers to the Philistine lord Achish for shelter. Can you imagine that, Eliab? He sought shelter with our enemies! I can hardly believe this is my son, my youngest, who fights with the king and hides with those killers. Even if he thought it acceptable to be with them, how could he have possibly thought they would have him, after what he has done against them?

He was wrong in thinking that the Philistines would trust him. Although he spoke little of it, when we met him at the cave of Adullam some of the men with him told us proudly of the escape they managed from Achish's court when things went wrong.

David's brothers went to the cave to see him too, but they have not stayed with him. In part they are jealous of his adventures (my Eliab especially so), in part afraid of the king, in part unsure of where David's ambitions will take him. But others are not held back by these or any other reasons! Many have been gathering there at the cave, unattractive men I was happy to be away from: malcontents, troublemakers, those with quarrels against the king or anyone else. They look to David to right all wrongs. And he accepts their service!

Whatever he is going to do – he says he looks to God for guidance! – Saul would certainly seek him in Bethlehem, so I have agreed to come back to the home of my ancestor until things settle down between him and the king. David cannot stay in that cave, because it's known all through Israel that he's there. I don't know where he will go or what will happen to him.

My friend, did we not think when our children were being born that they would be the joy of our old age? What has happened to that dream?

I wanted a good life for my youngest son. When he left for Saul's court I was sad to lose him. He seemed so young. Yet I also hoped that he might find a life there more suited to him than shepherding flocks on our farm. There was a strange capacity in him that the sheep would never appreciate! For several years I thought all was well. His reputation as a warrior and a courtier grew and reached us at Bethlehem. But now all appears lost and he runs for his life – and I run for mine because of him!

I fervently hope that God will be with him, because there's little encouragement from his circumstances or from those who serve him. Perhaps the Holy One will prosper him, as Samuel promised years ago. The prophet Gad is with him and no one has ever spoken a word against *his* devotion to the Lord!

I do not know when we will return to the farm. Take what you can from our fields for your use when you pass. Send word to us when you can.

Jesse

1.19 Water from Bethlehem's Well
Joab (at Adullam) writes to his mother, Zeruiah (at Bethlehem)

Dearest Mother,
We've found your brother here in this hiding place. Whether it really is a good place to hide we may soon find out. So many people know he's here that it may not be safe for long. As you suggested, my brothers and I have volunteered as officers in his service. Many others are doing the same thing. Some of them are impressive warriors. Others simply need to get away from things in their lives, and David provides an opportunity for that.

Whatever their background, he wins the kind of respect from them that you predicted we would find. A stunning example of this occurred a few days ago.

We are limited in our ability to get out of this stronghold and move around the country, because of both Saul and the Philistine raiding parties. The Philistines were in the valley between us last week, blocking us from getting to you in Bethlehem. David was restless. He hates being penned up by someone else's choices. He finally voiced his frustrations by saying he'd like a drink of water from the well at the gate to Bethlehem. While I'm sure he did want the water, it was really just an expression of how he felt his freedom was limited.

But three of the chiefs of his company took him at his word. Later in the evening they left the camp without telling him. They sneaked to the camp of the Philistines, and through it, and got some water from the well in Bethlehem to bring back to David. On their way back through the Philistine camp they were discovered and had to fight to get out. One of them was wounded, and they say they left two of the enemy bleeding on the ground. Then they ran to get clear before they were caught.

By the time they returned, everyone knew something was happening because of the noise in the Philistine camp. But we had no idea what it was until they showed up gasping for breath and showing off the skin of water they'd brought for David.

Any commander who could generate that kind of dedication would be impressive, but the truly impressive part was still to come. The officers crowded around David's tent to tell him the story and see him drink the water obtained at such risk. When he heard what had happened, he took the skin but he would not drink. Instead he said that he could not drink water obtained at the risk of his warriors' lives. He took the skin, spoke an oath to God, and poured the water onto the ground as a sacrifice to him.

The company was shocked into silence. I thought at first that the men would cry out against this waste. It almost seemed that David was treating the risk taken by his warriors as a small thing, that even though they had got the water for him, he would not accept it. But instead of being angry, the three were in awe. They bowed before David and said they were honoured that he so well understood the dedication they had for him and for his cause.

David turned away and entered his tent without another word. Nobody moved for a few moments, and then they all left silently as well. By the next evening every person in the stronghold had heard the story. Many wineskins were emptied around the campfires as the men toasted the three warriors, but they also toasted David for his care for his men.

His longing for water from that well we all know was almost childish, petulant. But men risked their lives to respond to it. And then he did something so unexpected and humble that the men's loyalty to him was only strengtlened. As you said, he can surprise.

We are more able to move about now that the raiding party has headed back to the coast. I will write again when there is something more than thirst and restlessness to describe.

Your obedient son,
Joab

1.20 Saul Slays Priests Allied with David
Abiathar the priest (at Adullam) writes to Samuel the prophet (at Ramah)

Master,
Blessed be the Lord, god of my fathers.

I have heard before of the horrors of war, but I had not seen them for myself. I had not seen the destruction the anger of a king can bring about, or the sorrow that can come from a sword – or how quickly it can come.

My father, Ahimelech, had no idea, I am sure, of what was happening when the messengers came from King Saul to our home at Nob. I say "messengers," but it was really a war band, and they did not come seeking for the priest only but his entire family. This was strange to be sure but not yet a sign of danger. The king has been so agitated about many things in recent years that to be summoned unexpectedly to advise him – to soothe him, in truth – has been a not infrequent thing for my father.

But when we stood before the king, it became clear that this was an audience with a different purpose. Saul was screaming at his officers as we arrived. He said they did not care for him, they did not value the prosperity he has brought to the land, and they did not inform him of palace intrigues of which they are aware. In short, they did not take his cause against David ben-Jesse. His rage was beyond anything I have seen. He waved his sword in the faces of his own officers. I did not know at that point what might happen.

As soon as he saw us all entering, he turned his anger on my father. He questioned him about David's recent visit to Nob. Doeg, the king's shepherd, had accused my father of fomenting rebellion by arming David and supplying him with provisions, and also of seeking the word of the Lord on David's behalf. But when David had visited us, although I know my father had suspicions, nothing was said about his flight from the court. It was not until later that we learned he had fled to Gath of the Philistines and then back to our own land to Adullam, as is now widely known among the people of the land.

Saul was really yelling out accusations rather than questions. He would not allow my father to complete his answers. It was clear that the answers didn't matter. Saul had decided what he intended to do before we arrived.

In spite of my father's claims of innocence, the king pronounced sentence on him: death to him and my grandfather's entire household! I was stunned, as were the king's own guards. They would not execute such a rash sentence so hastily given against servants of the Holy One.

Doeg, though, has no such scruples. The faith of Israel means little to him, and the favour of the king means a great deal. He chose to please the king and began a bloodbath I could not believe. My grandfather's family and household stood unarmed and defenseless and died where they stood.

The shocking attack – killing the Lord's priests! – stunned everyone present. Then the screams began and they were overwhelming. The blood spurting from the bodies of my family made me sick. I fell to my knees while Doeg did his killing. Even the king's guards were unable to respond at first.

I knew only that I must get the ancient sacred ephod the priest wears in his duties away from there so that Saul could not desecrate it, even if it meant abandoning my family. I took the robe and in the confusion fled from the king's presence. I alone escaped! The massacre was so great that I am sure I was not missed. I hid in Gibeah that night. The next day, yesterday, I sought shelter with David at Adullam.

I am sick with shock and sorrow. Why did this tragedy happen to my family? I cannot think clearly. And what has happened to King Saul? How can the Lord let his servant act in this unspeakably evil way?

In years past I have heard from my father the word you passed on to him, that the Lord has chosen David to be his ruler over Israel. I have committed my life to that word, coming here to a band of outcasts. I was pleased to meet Gad here. His presence gives me some assurance that I have sought protection in the right place. But the future is uncertain. The life I expected at Nob is gone forever. With David all is unknown. We cannot even stay here but must leave now that Saul knows where David is hiding.

I pray that the Lord, the God of my fathers, will go with us and guide us. Will the Lord protect us? My father was a faithful man, yet the Lord did not protect his life or family. Will the Lord protect me?

Master, you are a wise man. You know the ways of God. You know the ways of the king. I am with David. Please send any advice or instructions that you have for me. I know that you will talk with God about these matters.

Sincerely,
Abiathar

1.21 Doeg's Aspirations
Doeg, Saul's shepherd (at Nob), writes to his brother Ram (at Gibeah)

Ram,

At last the king is noticing me! I have done him a great service that no one else in his company would do.

King Saul sent to Nob yesterday in his search for David, who has been cleverly successful in escaping every time the king has tried to capture or kill him. David has fled from the court and we are after him. It was I myself who told Saul that David had been at Nob, and that he had been given provisions and weapons there by the priests. I happened to be there the day that David arrived, and I quickly went to Saul.

I hate David. My position as the king's shepherd should be an important one. I have large responsibilities for the flocks and for providing for the court and the army. But my influence was undermined while David was at court.

He is everywhere, always noticed, always praised. And his guile! He pretends not to want this glory. The people and even others at court have made him a hero. He is the great warrior and musician who was once a shepherd himself! The stories they tell about him make him larger than life. I am a shepherd too, but I am ignored.

So I was eager to tell Saul what I had learned when David visited, and eager to go back to Nob when he sent messengers searching for information about David.

We took the old priest and his family to Saul at Gibeah. When we arrived there, Saul was in a rage. He could scarcely control himself as he questioned the old priest. And when he was not satisfied with the answers he received, he screamed that he wanted the priest and all his family killed.

None of the warriors would move against the priests. They had more fear of God and his servants than of Saul. But those superstitions mean nothing to me. I gladly ignored them in order to be the one who did the king's bidding. I killed as many of them as I could find. We think that at least one of the sons escaped, but we will hunt him down. I returned to Nob with some of Saul's warriors and destroyed the entire town.

Saul's fury over David will drive him on in this search. And now he knows that I am the only one in the court who is driven by the same anger. The generals were weak in this matter, and I was strong.

Doeg

1.22 David Drives Back the Philistines
Abiathar the priest (at Keilah) writes to Samuel the prophet (at Ramah)

Master,
Blessed be God, the Lord of the hosts of Israel.

You know the mixed feelings I have about the ancient ephod. I want to serve the Lord, to be humble before him as he gives his words. At the same time it is exciting, a potential source of pride to be the keeper of the ephod, to receive the Lord's oracle through it, to be the one who speaks for God! Yet I am also afraid. I fear the power of the god who speaks to me and through me, and I know I must not hide his word from his people.

You have asked me at other times to explain to you how the ephod works. I know you would like to know this secret of the Lord, just as you know so many others. But, my master, I remain unable to fully describe it to you. All I know is that when I wear that ancient robe and am asked a question to put to the Lord, I know the answer that he wants to give. There is a certainty that I cannot explain. And I still do not know why this comes to me, as it did to my father, and not to someone more worthy than I. I do not know why God does not speak through you this way, master.

I am thankful, though, that he has chosen to speak through me to David. It reassures me that what I have done in coming to David is right. Certainly it was necessary to go *somewhere*, else Doeg would have killed me. The Lord's ways are not simple – serving him seems to mean serving the enemy of the anointed king!

Master, you and my other teachers did not prepare me for this. Perhaps the world was simpler when I studied with you. Or perhaps some of my teachers did not understand the Lord as well as they thought. For some the world had only simple choices – between the good and the evil. But I see much harder choices. Saul is God's king over God's chosen nation. David is an outlaw. Yet Saul has killed God's priests, and David grants protection.

And even David is not a man who allows simple choices. When he was told of the Philistine raids on Keilah in Judah, I thought he might ignore them. It would seem strange to seek shelter with the Philistines in Gath and then fight against them in Keilah. But he is a man of surprises – as the Lord is a God of surprises! When I used the ephod to ask about going against the Philistines I did not expect God to answer at all, and certainly not to answer telling David to go to battle.

The men do not have the faith that David shows. They did not want to go, even with the word from the Lord. When David asked a second time, I felt that he was going beyond what the Lord would accept. But the second request convinced the men, as apparently David and God had known that it would.

Master, I pray that the Lord will give me wisdom and patience in this difficult service into which he has brought me. What will Achish do when he learns of this?

My life here is so unlike what I expected. I wish you could visit us here so that Gad and I could speak with you. But I know your strength is failing, and soon the Lord will take you to himself. Perhaps it is a time to be well clear of this world.

In humility,
Abiathar

1.23 Saul Pursues David
Jonathan, Saul's son (at Gibeah), writes to his uncle Ner (at Jericho)

Dear Uncle,
It is a pleasure to me to help David. It makes me feel part of something with meaning. I have been to the desert to see him, and I was shocked by the conditions in which he lives. He has no home, always needing to be ready to move quickly, surrounded by such a strange mixture of outcasts and heroes, struggling always to find provisions for them.

I'm not surprised he is afraid. Any sensible person would be, and certainly an experienced general can sensibly realize when his force is outmatched. What gives me hope for David – for his life, for his blessing – is not the resources he has managed to gather together because, as he knows, these resources are nothing against those of the king. He has neither the army nor the political strength that my father has.

What David has is a promise from God. That promise is what he must cling to. I have reminded him of this. I have made a covenant with him that we will act as though this promise is true – he by expecting to be king, I by expecting not to be.

As always now, my father tells me nothing of his plans. But I have learned that he knows where David is hiding, and will go there himself. I pray that the Lord will be faithful to his own word that he will be with David to protect his life.

Uncle, my father neglects much of the work of being king because of this obsession with David. This course puts the nation at risk. If you were to advise him of his responsibilities, he might listen to you as he has in the past.

With respect,
Jonathan

1.24 David Escapes Saul's Pursuit
Abner, Saul's general (at Maon), writes to his father, Ner (at Jericho)

Dear Father,
Today we once again engaged with Philistine raiders. Will the threat from them never end? In this battle we again were successful. In our hills they lose the advantage of their weapons

and armour. I believe that Israel could deal with this menace decisively and end it if the king would give his attention to it rather than to David ben-Jesse. I have told him this again after today's success. And again I saw the rage that drives him at any mention of ben-Jesse. He cannot concentrate on defeating the Philistines because he considers another a more threatening enemy.

It was only with difficulty, in fact, that the king was convinced to break off his pursuit of David to deal with the Philistines. He knew he almost had David in his hands and was not easily turned. But even in his rage he can see that the people of Israel will not tolerate a king who ignores a present threat to deal with a potential future one.

As it was, we had to force march from Maon to engage the Philistines, and the host is now tired, unready for repulsing another raid – I hope there will not soon be one. We had arrived in Maon based on information obtained from Ziph about David's location. Saul now knows better than simply to go where David is rumoured to be. That slippery one can move so quickly. When we attempted to verify the intelligence we had, David was discovered in Maon, and it was on the mountain of Maon that we were closing in on him when the Philistines struck.

We have been close to David so many times! I too wanted him this time. Not that I think he is a real threat, but we need to get Saul's attention back to the real issues of national security. I am more determined than ever to find and eliminate David! There is a report tonight that he has been seen at En-Gedi. If this can be confirmed, we'll go there. He has few choices out in the desert. He may well know the desert better than I do, but there are few sources of water and he must stay near them.

If we do go to En-Gedi I will look for an opportunity to visit you in Jericho. I would value some peace, and some calm talk with you.

With love,
Abner

1.25 David Lets Saul Live
Abner, Saul's general (at Gibeah), writes in the annals of the army

This note is a formal record of the complaint I have made to the king. The reckless pursuit of David ben-Jesse has implications for national security: the king neglects real and present dangers to pursue his personal agenda. This has political consequences: the people will not support a king who does not deal with pressing national problems. Without the support of the people, the king is no king, and Israel will revert to the chaos and anarchy that preceded the establishment of the kingdom. And now this obsessive pursuit of ben-Jesse has put the king's own life at risk.

In his eagerness to engage David's force today – which we outnumbered by three thousand to six hundred! – the king did not take proper precautions. He went alone to relieve himself in a cave without guards and without a prior security check. David and some of his men were there in the dark, and the king was completely unaware of their presence. He could have been killed. Fortunately, all David did was surreptitiously remove a corner of the king's cloak.

When we had resumed our march and were further down the hill, David emerged and told what had happened in the hearing of all our men. He claimed himself to be unworthy of the king's attention, and in any case uninterested in harming the king. He invoked the Lord as judge between himself and the king.

Saul was embarrassed and knew he was to blame. He was overcome at the danger he had just escaped and his own heedlessness. At David's invocation of the Lord, he agreed to give up the pursuit.

David and his men left to return to the stronghold of En-Gedi that they have made a temporary headquarters. From my perspective, that is a good place for them to be. There is little nearby that they can threaten (although there is no evidence that they would, even if given the opportunity), and they are far enough away from Gibeah to be out of the king's way.

My formal recommendation to the king has been that this withdrawal and disengagement be of indefinite duration. The king and the army have more important things to do than to hunt the king's son-in-law – who has done no harm to the kingdom or to the king – in his native Judean desert!

1.26 Abner's Complaint

Abner, Saul's general (at Gibeah), writes to his father, Ner (at Jericho)

Dear Father,
I have made a formal recommendation to Saul to cease from pursuing David. While he has agreed, I'm afraid he may not maintain his resolve. It can be extremely difficult to be a senior minister in

the government of a family member! If he were not my cousin, and if I were not concerned for his welfare and the family name, I should have resigned this wretched post by now. But I stay because I think that our family and the tribe of Benjamin could come into disrepute if the king were left unchecked.

In haste,
Abner

1.27 The Death of Samuel
Abiathar the priest (at Ramah) writes in his journal

Blessed be the Lord of Israel, who is mysterious in his ways.

Today we buried Samuel. This is the end of an important era in Israel's history. We called him a prophet, but he was so revered and respected in Israel that he was almost a ruler. He linked us back to old ways and old days. All of us who were close to him knew that he preferred the Israel of his childhood to the Israel of his old age.

One of the most important changes he saw was the change from rule by religious leaders to rule by a king. Of course Samuel was the one who anointed Saul to be the first king, but the stories of his uneasiness with that are still told. I am sure that Saul has resented Samuel's reluctance during all the years he has been king.

Samuel would have preferred that religious leaders continue to rule in Israel as was the pattern for many generations. But the people wanted a king, and God wanted to give them one. Poor Saul, to be that first king, unwanted by the leader who preceded him and who continued to be a strong force in the nation. Samuel and Saul were at odds for so long that the tension generated by their differences became almost a normal part of the life of our people.

There were other ways too in which Samuel preferred the past. He was continually preaching about the faithfulness to God in past generations and the need for repentance in the present one. He deplored the rapidly increasing trade in iron tools and weapons and hated the awfulness of war and bloodshed that these weapons have made possible. This has been especially true as the Philistines have attacked from the coast with chariots and sharp swords.

Because of these things, many of the people thought of Samuel as an angry old man. But he was not that, and the burial ceremony today made that clear. He was a man deeply devoted to God. He gave his life to service for God and for the nation, just as his mother anticipated when he was born. He was a man deeply devoted to righteousness. He wanted the people of God to live as God intended. He wanted this not because he wished to make their lives small and uninteresting but because he believed it would make their lives fulfilled and exciting. He often told us, his students, that he could wish for nothing better for us than the fulfilment that he himself had in his life of service. It is a great loss to Israel to have him gone. His devotion to God and to righteous living will be sorely missed.

Where he will be missed most, though, will be in discussions of Israel's future. For decades Samuel was the one who identified the things that needed doing, and the people – the prophets and priests, other officials, the current king, and David, secretly anointed to succeed Saul – who could do them. Those of us he has left behind will have to take up his role.

All this is what his death means for our nation. But for me? Samuel was my beloved teacher, as he was for so many others. No other teacher demanded so much or thought me capable of so much. No other encouraged or cajoled me as he did. I feel as if an era has ended. The past, because it is fully known, always seems so much safer and more secure than the future. I wonder about the future even more now. And I have a sense of responsibility for it that I never felt when Samuel was alive.

I am pleased that Gad is in the service of David, as am I. I would not want to be there alone, and losing Samuel makes me feel somewhat alone already. I know I should be comforted by the presence of God himself, but I need people of God around me to make that presence real.

1.28 A Restraint Removed

Jonathan, Saul's son (at Ramah), writes to his uncle, Ner (at Jericho)

Dear Uncle,
Many came to bury Samuel, mourning the end of an age in Israel. My father struggled to control himself in front of the people. On

the one hand he was pleased to see his frequent adversary gone. He hopes that the threat Samuel uttered years ago that the kingdom would pass to another will have been proven to be idle. With Samuel gone he hopes to destroy David and consolidate his power.

On the other hand, he knew he must behave as a grieving monarch who has lost an advisor widely respected by the people. I could see that he was barely able to restrain himself through the ceremony and was anxious to be off again to hunt for David.

I fear that the danger to David and to Israel is mounting. Samuel was a restraining influence on my father simply by his existence. Now the king's anger and jealousy will have free reign. I doubt that Abner can hold him back.

With great respect,
Jonathan

1.29 Spying on Saul
Joab (at Ramah) writes to his mother, Zeruiah (at Bethlehem)

Dear Mother,
I attended Samuel's funeral to observe Saul, disguised as a farm labourer so that Saul's people would not recognize me. The king was extremely agitated. I expect him now to hunt down David with no restraint on his fury. He left quickly with his personal guard for the desert. I have had to be careful here, and so have learned little of specific advantage. But David must be told of the likelihood of renewed pursuit. I must hurry to him.

With love and respect,
Joab

1.30 David Meets Nabal and Abigail
Abigail (at Carmel) writes to her sister Sarah (at Bethel)

Dear Sister,
I have met the notorious David ben-Jesse. Since Samuel's death he has been in the desert near here with his thousand (actually, about six hundred men), and we have heard many stories about him

even though we have never seen him. My Nabal has little respect for him, a man without property and connections. But our chief shepherd has told me – and Nabal! – that David's men protected our sheep against both human and animal raiders when the flocks were near David's encampment. So of course Nabal has been keeping flocks there to have the benefit of David's protection.

Yesterday David sent to ask for some recognition of the help that he has given us. His band is without flocks or lands, dependent on the generosity of others for provisions. But Nabal refused to send anything. I'm sure he thought this another crafty piece of business on his part – to have the protection for our flocks but pay nothing for it. He threw David's messengers out and celebrated his advantage with a feast, getting drunk again.

Our servants knew David would not accept this insult and told me the whole story. I'm tired of protecting my husband and covering up for him, Sarah. But it had to be done again, so I took provisions and quickly went to David. It's well that I hurried, because I met him and a large band already coming toward us, armed for a fight that our household surely would have lost.

I can't convey to you the impression that ben-Jesse made on me because he is not easy to understand or describe. He is obviously a great warrior. We have all heard of his exploits, yet he now leads an embarrassing collection of misfits. He himself has a confident way with the men and with others – certainly with me. He looks, moves, and talks like a general comfortable with command, expecting to be heard and obeyed. But he was not sharp or harsh with his men, just direct and expectant. Some of his commanders are also obviously accustomed to power and success.

The men they lead cannot make their way in their own villages and so have fled to David. Some of them are ragged and dirty – and they smell. The conditions under which they live in the desert are hard to imagine. With no claim to any land of their own, they have no easy access to water.

Three in particular who stood near David were evidently respected by the others. All that I could make out about them was their size and apparent strength. They had the largest arms and shoulders I'd ever seen. They did not speak the entire time but stood by David as if to protect him from me and my servants. Perhaps their real function was to strike a note of fear; my servants seemed terrified of them. As we returned home afterwards, they told me that each of the three had earned his position near David by single-handedly killing large numbers in hand-to-hand combat in battle. David seemed at ease with them, treating them with respect but almost taking them for granted.

Others, though, appeared to have nothing of value to offer. Many looked to me like malcontents, perhaps hoping to find in David someone to change their lives for the better. Again, he seemed to be easily accepting of all these people around him.

He makes strange choices not only in his soldiers but in his strategy. Though he has the support of the people of Judah in his conflict with Saul, he flees rather than fight. Yet he was sufficiently moved by Nabal's lesser affront to be ready to respond with force.

I begged forgiveness for our household, offered the provisions I had hurriedly taken with me, and suggested that David should let God deal with Nabal rather than force men to do it. This seemed a good approach to take, since David reputedly refuses to fight Saul because Saul is God's anointed. He heard my words and took them to heart, even thanking me for them. I felt there was a oneness of spirit between us.

My husband, though, was not so accepting when he was sober and I told him the mistake he had made and how once again I covered up for him. This marriage is far from what I expected. I don't know how much more of Nabal's abuse I am willing to endure. I don't believe it has ended yet.

With love,
Abigail

1.31 David's Family Wonders about Him
Asahel (at Carmel) writes to his mother, Zeruiah (at Bethlehem)

Dear Mother,
I write in haste, as I have been sent to find provisions for the company. But I thought you would want to know this.

Perhaps your brother is more astute than you have thought. We have been giving protection out in the desert to the flocks of a local noble of some standing named Nabal. When David asked for provisions as payment for that protection, Nabal refused. But his wife, Abigail, supplied us without his agreement. She and David were drawn to each other; this was clear to all of us as we watched them talking. Within days Nabal had died, perhaps from shock at learning all that had transpired. In any case, now David has taken Abigail as his own wife!

She is an intelligent, beautiful woman and politically brings him considerable respectability in this area. He retains Ahinoam of Jezreel as wife as well, also an alliance of some importance. We have recently learned that Saul has given Michal to be the wife of Paltiel ben-Laish, so that David is no longer the king's son-in-law. Thus this new match with Abigail will help to rebuild his political base.

Of course he has not referred to the importance of these alliances, but they are important, as you have pointed out before. Have we underestimated him?

With love,
Asahel

1.32 David Spares Saul Again
Abishai (at Ziph) writes to his mother, Zeruiah (at Bethlehem)

Dearest Mother,
We have given away another excellent opportunity to deal with Saul! The Ziphites again betrayed our location to him, so we moved from the hills down to the Desert of Ziph. When Saul came to find us, David went to a spot where he could overlook the king's camp, and decided to go into the camp himself.

He asked for a volunteer to go with him, so I offered, hoping to find a way to force his hand. The king's army was tired after a hard day's march pursuing us. They had no idea how close they were! Clouds covered the moon, so the night was dark. The fires in their camp were allowed to burn low, because there were few with the energy to keep them going. Many of the soldiers on the night watch, even many of the king's personal guards, fell asleep. We were able to creep right to Saul's side without disturbing anyone! I urged David to end this foolishness by killing him. But again he would not, only taking Saul's spear and water jug.

When we were safely away, he stood in the open and taunted Abner with this failure of security in the king's camp. He spoke directly to Saul too, repeating that he has no desire to harm him.

Saul was convinced once again to leave off his pursuit and go home.

But we remain here in this desert, away from the centres of power, apparently content to wait. Why do we wait, and for what? For Saul to die of old age? I wish this brother of yours were more willing to act, Mother.

With love and frustration,
Abishai

1.33 David Makes an Alliance with the Philistines
Ahinoam (at Ziklag) writes to her sister Milcah (at Jezreel)

My sister,
You wonder what it is like to be married to David ben-Jesse, do you? I'll tell you two things now, and more when I next see you. Do not rush into marriage before then.

First, it is terrifying. Since I have been David's wife, I have lived with his band, first in the desert, but now we have taken shelter with the Philistines. This is all to avoid King Saul. When he chased us in the desert, his forces far outnumbered ours so that I was afraid we would be caught and killed. And this by our own overlord and king in our own land! Now we have escaped that pursuit, but David takes great risks with Achish, the Philistine lord of Gath. We now live here in Ziklag as his vassals.

David tells Achish that the spoils he captures come from raiding the towns of Israel, but this is untrue. Instead, he is raiding the towns of the enemies of Israel. So he is keeping us "safe" with Achish by lying about what he does. I am afraid that this deception cannot be continued and that we will be slain by our own host and new-found overlord in a foreign land.

David does not tell *me* what he has in mind in all of this. The developments are always coming as surprises. He seems to be very comfortable expressing himself to the Lord in his songs, but he does not express his thoughts or explain his behaviour to those around him. The men of his thousand do not seem to mind. They follow him almost without question, expecting him to be thinking in ways they cannot understand. But I long to know more of what is in his mind.

But the second thing about being married to David ben-Jesse is that he makes life full. When I am with him I feel truly alive. It is as though he pursues life, to find it and consume it. Some of this is not what I would choose were I alone, and some of it is not easy to enjoy. Yet having now experienced it, I would not choose to live without it.

Does your intended husband bring you this fullness? I know we have been taught to value someone who can provide well for a wife and a family, and that is surely a good thing. But there is more that we can ask for too.

Love,
Ahinoam

1.34 The Philistines Reject David
Ahinoam (at Ziklag) writes to her sister Milcah (at Jezreel)

Dear Sister,
I've not heard from you in the months since I last wrote. My caution about your intended marriage was not intended to offend you, although I fear that it has. Or perhaps you do not write because you are angry at our being in Philistia. I don't know. Offended or not, you are my sister, and I must warn you now. David has just sent word from a council of the Philistine lords. They are planning to attack Jezreel! You must prepare. I would like you to flee, but at least you must warn the city and be prepared. The Philistines are bringing a united force against Israel this time, hoping to do more damage than in the sporadic raids of the past years. You must get word to King Saul.

David knows I am writing to you. He advised it because he is angry. Yet he is also pleased, I think, that the other Philistine lords were so wary of his presence that they forced our overlord Achish to keep him and his men out of the battle force. He will now return to us here. I pray that this note will reach you in time. One of David's men will bring it to you and then return, I hope, with news that you were able to protect yourselves.

With love, in haste and fear,
Ahinoam

1.35 David Destroys Foreign Raiders
Abiathar the priest (at Ziklag) writes to Gad the prophet (at Ramah)

Fellow-servant,
Greetings in the name of the Lord, the one who gives and guards our lives.

Our God *must* be with David, my friend, because only the divine one could turn disaster into victory as has happened here.

David and his thousand (he still uses that Israelite military term, even here in Philistia) had been with the Philistine lord Achish. I was with them, because David always wants me near him with the ephod. When we returned to Ziklag after having had David's offer to fight alongside the men of Achish refused, we found that our families and possessions were gone. They had been carried off by an Amalekite raiding party inflicting on us what the thousand has often inflicted on others. The men were angry with David, saying that he seemed more concerned with his relationship to Achish than our loyalties to our own people in Israel or the protection of families and flocks.

In spite of the evidence from the amount of food they had consumed that the raiding party was very large, David had me inquire of God whether he should chase after it. To me it seemed audacious to consider such a thing, and to consider involving the Lord in it! Surely the raid against us was God's punishment for our willingness to fight against Israel? Yet the oracle came, and David was assured of victory. When we reached Besor Ravine some of the men were too tired to continue, having just completed a forced march back from the Philistine council. David left two hundred there with our supplies and continued on with only four hundred. I wondered at the wisdom of that decision.

But his judgment that we were close to the raiders and should press on was correct. The scouts soon returned with a slave of one of the raiding captains. The man had been abandoned without help or food when he became ill. For a promise of protection, he was willing to tell about the company and show us where they were camped. This band had raided in several places in Israel and elsewhere; there were many of them, and they had amassed a large amount of booty on which they were feasting when we came on them.

David's zeal was once again contagious! It's amazing to see how he leads his men in these situations. They fought with skill and fury, destroying almost all the raiders and recovering all of our people and possessions unharmed and a good deal more besides.

The wives and children of our men were overjoyed. They had believed the force that had taken them was so strong they would never be rescued. David's skill was so appreciated that the men designated all the flocks (beyond our own) that were captured as his personal spoil.

When we returned to Besor, some of the men who had fought wanted to separate out all the spoils for themselves, returning only the wives and children of those who had stayed behind. But David would not agree to this and shared the plunder among all, saying that those who stayed behind also contributed to the victory by guarding our remaining possessions. This was so unexpectedly generous that, apart from a few troublemakers, the men and their families of both those who fought and those who stayed behind were praising David for it. They were speaking of him as a great leader and telling each other how much better it is to serve him than any other commander.

David then took his own share and divided it to be sent to the elders of Judah in many cities and towns. He presented it to them as "plunder of the Lord's enemies." My friend, he is an amazing person. A week ago we were mustered to fight against Israel, but now he has sent gifts to Judah. His fame and the respect for him there will have grown by this rather than being diminished, as would have happened if they had learned what he apparently intended to do! And a few days ago the thousand were almost in rebellion, but now they are once again praising his skill in battle, his courage, and his generosity.

Out of impending failure he has made success. Is he just an opportunistic schemer, or is the Lord indeed here? If the Lord is here, what is ahead for David, for you and for me as servants of the Lord, and for the nation?

Hurry back to us. I miss the chance to talk these things over with you. Sometimes it is not easy to know the ways of God.

Under the mercy,
Abiathar

1.36 The Death of Saul
Abishai (at Ziklag) writes to his mother, Zeruiah (at Bethlehem)

Dear Mother,

Has this news reached you yet? Surely it must have. We have just heard today that King Saul is dead, along with his son, the prince and heir, Jonathan. What do you think this can mean for us, our family, and especially for David? I cannot predict what he will do next.

A foreigner – an Amalekite – brought us the news. He had been present (I do not know why) at the battle on Mount Gilboa between Israel's army under Saul and the combined Philistine forces. It is even probable that he was with or near King Saul when he died in that battle. He claimed, in fact, to have killed Saul at his own request, because Saul was suffering from wounds and was sure to be captured and tortured. The man certainly had Saul's armbands and headbands to support his claim, and he knew enough about the state of things in Israel and Judah that he brought these tokens to David.

But he did not know David as well as he thought he did.

His story seemed unlikely, and many of us suspected him of lying, at least about having delivered the fatal blow to Saul. Even so, David ordered that he be killed, for he had "destroyed the anointed of the Lord," David said. I suppose even if the story he told was false, the man was conspiring against the kingdom of the Lord by his lies. And perhaps David was still angry at what the foreign raiders had done to Ziklag, so being an Amalekite was not healthy.

David then disappeared into his own tent for several hours. When he reappeared, it was with a new song, a lament for Saul and Jonathan. He wanted it written down and taught to all the men of Judah. The song makes much of Saul and does not mention the trouble between Saul and David at all. There are also some moving words about his old friendship with Jonathan, which we might have expected since the two of them were once extremely close. Does he actually think like this, Mother, or is he extremely subtle?

You have surely known of Saul's death longer than I, Mother, and have surely been thinking about the implications. Who will be king now with both Saul and Jonathan gone? The other princes are insignificant, unable to lead. Will the alliance between the north and the south hold? I hope you will send me your thoughts and your advice.

With love,
Abishai

1.37 David's Meditation: Lament for Saul and Jonathan
David writes at Ziklag

> Your glory, O Israel, lies slain upon your high places!
>   How the mighty have fallen!
> Tell it not in Gath,
>   proclaim it not in the streets of Ashkelon;
> or the daughters of the Philistines will rejoice,
>   the daughters of the uncircumcised will exult.
>
> You mountains of Gilboa,
>   let there be no dew or rain upon you,
>   nor bounteous fields!
> For there the shield of the mighty was defiled,
>   the shield of Saul, anointed with oil no more.
>
> From the blood of the slain,
>   from the fat of the mighty,
> the bow of Jonathan did not turn back,
>   nor the sword of Saul return empty.
>
> Saul and Jonathan, beloved and lovely!
>   In life and in death they were not divided;
> they were swifter than eagles,
>   they were stronger than lions.
>
> O daughters of Israel, weep over Saul,
>   who clothed you with crimson, in luxury,
>   who put ornaments of gold on your apparel.
>
> How the mighty have fallen
>   in the midst of the battle!

Jonathan lies slain upon your high places.
   I am distressed for you, my brother Jonathan;
greatly beloved were you to me;
   your love to me was wonderful,
      passing the love of women.

How the mighty have fallen,
   and the weapons of war perished!

2 Foundation

Zadok the Scribe's Commentary

In the first group of documents there is some uncertainty around David. His time with the Philistines, for example, was difficult even for his father to understand. But the lament for Saul and Jonathan seems to come from a man who genuinely mourned them, even though some others suspected otherwise.

After the death of King Saul, the kingdom split in two. The tribe of Judah crowned David as their king. But the remainder of the tribes stayed together under the rule of Saul's son, Ishbaal. This man was not a strong king, but he did have the able support of Saul's general, Abner, who became in fact the real power in the kingdom of Israel.

There was war between the two kingdoms. David did not seem to pursue it vigorously. But his general, Joab (also his nephew), was convinced that all the problems of the realm could be resolved if the kingdoms were reunited under David. The strife between the two kingdoms became a personal vendetta for Joab after Abner killed Joab's brother Asahel. Joab's feelings on this matter almost jeopardized the larger peace towards which David was apparently working.

All of the negotiations that were leading to a peaceful restoration of the kingdom came close to collapse. Abner's murder and the assassination of Ishbaal left David with a volatile situation which he skilfully managed. Both the real leader and the nominal leader of Israel were dead, with David implicated. But he managed to avoid the blame and negotiated directly with the elders of the nation to achieve the peace that Abner had begun to arrange. David had now developed the political acumen required of a king.

The documents in the second group are from this time when David reigned over Judah, with the nation divided. Half of the documents are written by the generals of the two opposing camps, Joab and Abner. Joab writes to his mother, as in the earlier material. Abner writes to one of Saul's former concubines, Rizpah, whom he had come to love after Saul's death. David's wife, Michal, daughter of Saul, became an important symbol of the linkage being established between the two kingdoms and the two ruling houses. She writes about her anger at how she was treated.

Joab and Abner are strong men. Certainly Joab is ruthless. How can David base a rule as God's king on the foundation of the work of such a man? I had thought that a righteous kingdom would need a righteous foundation.

When the entire nation of Israel crowned David as their king, he was faced with a formidable challenge. It is one thing to have the leaders of the nation realize that a course of action is the best one open to them. It is quite another to have all the people affirm that what has been done is good for them and for their interests. Thus while David had successfully negotiated with the leaders of Israel, he now had to build a single nation again, a nation united under and committed to his leadership.

He set out to do two things. First, he needed a capital city. For many reasons, he chose Jerusalem. This city had stood against the Israelites when they conquered the land God had given them, and in David's time it was still a free city. David conquered it and made it the capital of his kingdom.

Second, he needed to unite the people in their religious commitment to the Lord, the God of our ancestors. He did this by bringing into his new capital the Ark that Moses had made in the desert and that had been largely neglected (although not by a few faithful priests). This was not accomplished without controversy and difficulty, as the documents in this group show.

I have presented one document here out of its chronological order. David's wife, Michal, had no children. Late in her life she wrote about this to her cousin, making clear that the cause for her barrenness lay in her conflict with David over bringing the Ark to Jerusalem. Consequently, I have put this letter together with other documents referring to that time.

2.01 David, King of Judah
Abigail (at Hebron) writes to her sister Sarah (at Bethel)

Dear Sister,
We've moved again, and it's safe now to visit us. I hope you will. I missed the family so much during the time we were hiding in the desert. David has brought his thousand from the desert to Hebron, and they have settled here with their families. I think we've at last found a home.

Since David does not tell me what he's doing in the way I had expected he would, I did not know he had planned to come here. But he had the idea of moving into some city of Judah and asked God to confirm his intention. God directed him to this one. With Saul gone, it's safe now for those in our own tribe of Judah to acknowledge us. Life in the desert was hard, so for David to look for a way out of that situation was not too surprising.

What did surprise me was that the elders of Judah came here to welcome David – and even made him king! I had hoped for him to become king at some point, but of the entire nation of Israel, not just one tribe. Since the rest of Israel is not involved in this business, it means splitting the kingdom, and probably civil war, I fear. We don't yet know what will happen to the kingship in Israel but expect someone from Saul's house to assume it. I am hoping the house of Saul will leave Judah alone so that we can live here peacefully and that David will be content to do so.

He has sent a commendation to the town of Jabesh Gilead for burying Saul. This might be simply acknowledging their deed, but it may also be the first step towards building a larger base of power in Israel. I pray that David will be content here and that we can raise our family in peace.

Whatever is to happen in the future, this is a good time to come, so please do. We have seen too little of each other while I have been in the desert.

I have some other good news, too: I am pregnant. Tell Mother, but do not tell any others. As I am carrying the child of the king, the announcement of the pregnancy and of the birth will become affairs of state.

Love,
Abigail

2.02 Civil War after Saul's Death
Joab (at Hebron) writes to his mother, Zeruiah (at Bethlehem)

Dearest Mother,
I write with terrible news, news I hate to deliver to you. My brother Asahel is dead, killed by that damned Abner.

It happened yesterday. Asahel, Abishai, and I were with a band of warriors when we met Abner at the pool of Gibeon. Abner has been increasingly bold in taking an open leadership position in Israel and its army. He still maintains the sham that Ishbaal ben-Saul is the rightful king, and that the army Abner leads supports the king. But in reality its senior general is ruling Israel!

Abner proposed a battle of champions to decide between us, rather than having all warriors in both groups fight. Since David had put me in charge of our party, I agreed to this. We each chose twelve men to represent us.

They were well matched, too well matched, I suppose. In fact, in each pair the matched warriors were so close in ability that each killed the other. Think of that: twelve pairs of matched warriors and twelve pairs of deaths. Champions as if for each of the twelve tribes of Israel, but twelve pairs of deaths with no resolution of the conflict. After all that fighting and killing designed to limit the bloodshed, the issue between us was still undecided.

In the fight between the two bands that followed this, we were winning. But Abner (may he be forever cursed!) and a few of his men escaped from the fighting. Asahel gave chase and caught up with him. Others of our band were close enough to see and hear what happened, but not close enough to help – Asahel was the fastest runner of us all.

Abner apparently warned Asahel to stop the chase or be killed (he said he could then not face me!), but of course Asahel would not stop. So as Asahel approached from behind, Abner with his amazing strength drove his spear handle back at Asahel as they both ran, and impaled him on the handle! My brother died immediately where he fell.

The men were shocked and stopped to deal with Asahel's body. But Abishai and I continued after Abner, hoping that together we might avenge our brother. Some of Abner's men stood with him as we approached, and he called out that we should give up the chase. Had we not been outnumbered so badly, we would have continued. But I saw we could not take him, so we turned back.

I swear to you, Mother, that I will have Abner's life for what he has done. I cannot bring Asahel to you again, but I will avenge him and bring you news of his killer's death. I will not rest until that has happened.

When we returned to Hebron, David was there to hear what happened. The one good that has come from today's sorrowful events is that he has formally confirmed me as general of his host. The job I have been doing unofficially is now mine. I hope you can take some comfort in this even on such a day of grief.

As soon as I have made arrangements here for the few days of our absence, Abishai and I will come to Bethlehem to be with you and to mourn our brother together.

Abner will burn in sheol for this, and I will send him there.

Your obedient son,
Joab

2.03 Abner Is Frustrated
Abner, Saul's general (at Hebron), writes to Rizpah (at Gibeah)

Dear one,
I will return tomorrow to the court. I send this on ahead because my warriors and I must rest here.

Today we met with Joab and a band of David's men. It was unexpected and dangerous and could have been disastrous. Joab is a fool! And his foolishness could provoke something none of us can control. While David seems willing to be king only in Judah (at least for now), Joab wants the nation reunited, with David as king of all Israel. And he believes that he can accomplish this through battle, with his army defeating mine. But it's not that simple, as I well know and as I suspect David does also.

To avoid a massive slaughter, we agreed to a battle of champions. But even that ended unexpectedly, as I will tell you when I return. When it was over, my men and I fled because I was still unwilling to engage with Joab's band.

But Joab's brother, Asahel, who could run like the wind, pursued us and would not give up the chase. I guarded the rear of my company, and after several attempts to have him withdraw, I was forced to kill him. Joab caught up with us, but by then he was well ahead of his own men, and I and mine outnumbered him. He turned back without a fight.

He will be even more dangerous now. His schemes to push David faster than he wants to be pushed, combined with his rage at this day's sad work, will drive him to foolishness. I must make careful plans to preserve peace. I wish that Ishbaal were the leader we need to keep the nation together and to establish Saul's dynasty. I want a life of peace with you and with the children we will have together.

Yours,
Abner

2.04 David's Family Expands
Ahinoam (at Hebron) writes to her sister Milcah (at Jezreel)

Sister,
There's to be yet another wife in this family, and one who could interfere with my plans.

We've been seven years in Hebron while David has been king of Judah. We have been comfortable here. Though there has been war, it has been elsewhere. David would not fight against Saul when Saul was king of Israel. But he has certainly been willing to fight against Ishbaal, and Joab has been encouraging the fighting. I know David wants to see the kingdom reunited.

While he has not said it to me, I believe that anointing by the prophets of the Lord is very important to him. Saul was anointed by Samuel to be king. And David himself was anointed. But Ishbaal was not: he assumed the kingdom as an inheritance from his father. David is not opposed to fighting someone who claims to be king, but he will not fight someone who has been chosen by the Lord. Of course, part of his purpose in this is that he wants others to be unwilling to attack the Lord's anointed king too, since now *he* is the anointed king.

Hebron has been safe and a good place for raising children. David has provided well for us here and has given me the son I longed for, Amnon, David's firstborn child. I believe my son should be the next king. And if David is able to keep stability in the kingdom and come to understand that the kingdom should be passed on in his family, Amnon *will* be king. David will certainly maintain a stable kingdom; he has been a good king for the people of Judah.

Of course, David has other wives and other children. I would rather that he had not made those choices, but I understand them. He needed to build alliances in many places and married to do so. Each of his other wives has also borne him a son. The boys play well together most of the time. Sometimes, though, Amnon and Absalom (the second son) fight and need to be separated from each other and from the other children. When this happens, rivalries among the wives become evident. Each one knows that David will eventually want to choose a successor as king, and each wants it to be her own son.

Now our lives will be even more complicated. David had Saul's daughter, Michal, as a wife when he was a young general in Saul's army. They separated when Saul drove David away, and Michal has had another husband. But David is now bringing her back as part of his negotiation to assume the kingship of all Israel. I certainly hope that he does not intend to try for a son with her, a son who as descendant of both David and Saul would have a strong claim to the throne. But David does not tell me his thinking on these matters.

Ahinoam

2.05 Abner Negotiates with David
Michal (at Hebron) writes to her cousin Marah (at Gibeah)

Dear cousin,

I know it's a long time since you've heard from me, though you've probably heard *about* me – my life seems to be lived in front of the entire nation. And you do seem to hear from me only when I'm in need. In so many of the difficulties in the Kish family, you are still the one who is called on to give comfort, and I desperately need comfort now. I'm not getting any from my husband (in name only!) and perhaps never will.

David demanded me back as his wife before he would make peace with the house of Saul. Another sham, that! In truth, it was before he would make peace with my father's general, my cousin Abner.

Though I have felt sorry for my young brother Ishbaal, I have known since before my father's death that he would not make a good king. Abner has been all the power in the realm of Israel these seven years. But Abner has grown tired of maintaining the illusion that Ishbaal rules. Abner has all the responsibility but none of the privileges of being king. He asked my brother for my father's concubine, Rizpah, daughter of Aish. He loves her, I think, but he did this also to assert his position in the kingdom by appearing to have the former king's harem. Ish has grown to like the title and the privileges of being king, even though he does not do the work, and he has rebuked Abner.

This has all resulted in Abner becoming angry enough to make an approach to David. They are now negotiating to re-unite the kingdom under David as sole king of Judah and Israel.

I had grown comfortable in my life with Paltiel ben-Laish. Although I was forced into marriage with him by my father, Paltiel loved me and did his best to make our life together happy and full. When David asked for me back, I hoped that it might be because he loved me as I have continued to love him. Leaving my marriage with Paltiel was hard, but I could bear it to return to David's love.

Yet David has not spoken of love to me. He has, in fact, barely spoken to me at all. Perhaps he has distrusted me since the days when my father hunted him, even though I tried to support him, hide him, and show my love for him. And the reports I hear of his negotiation with Abner tell only of his referring to the bride price he paid and to his legal claim on me.

I have loved David too much. My love for him trapped me. It caused me to rebel against my father. It caused me to stay alone while David hid in the wilderness (and married other wives). It caused me to long for him to come to me again through these years with Paltiel. It caused me to rejoice like a fool when he asked for me back.

But my love obviously cannot make David love me. I wonder if he only wanted me as a tie to the house of Saul. Perhaps he hopes for a child of our marriage to succeed him, with the aid of my father's supporters as well as from his own. I have longed for a child, but to embody the love between us, not as an agent in these kingdom conflicts. Whatever comes from this marriage, I fear it will not be brought about through love.

Cousin, I have written at this length to convince you of my need for you. It has not been easy to face my troubles and to write about them. I beg you to come to me.

I have been here in Hebron with David's company for a week. The situation is volatile. Abner has met with the elders of Israel, saying to them that they *want* to make David king and that he can help them. Imagine that! It must be true, else he would not have risked saying it. They too have felt the strain of this period with Ishbaal as a sham king. Abner now acts as liaison between David and Israel, and between David and our own tribe of Benjamin! The end of this must come soon. But a political resolution will not help me personally, I'm afraid.

I feel alone here, unwanted by the others in David's household, and ignored by David. I was his wife for only a few weeks before he fled from my father's court, and it may be that my role here will be purely symbolic. I've lost all of the relationships I knew as a girl. I've lost the only marriage of any duration that I have had.

I would like to be with someone who loves me and will not use me.

In need, again,
Michal

2.06 Abner Anticipates Success
Abner, Saul's general (at Hebron), writes to Rizpah (at Gibeah)

Dear one,
I write in haste. The war is ended, and our life is about to begin! I am about to leave David's court for the journey back to you but will send this note in advance by messenger.

I went to see the elders of Israel before coming here. All parties are in agreement that Ishbaal must step aside and that David will assume the rule of all Israel. Fortunately Joab was off on David's business elsewhere, so what was a complicated negotiation was at least conducted without the hot-heads present.

I had hoped after Saul's death to establish stability through Saul's lineage and thought Ishbaal could be the means of doing that. Most of the tribes had wanted that too. But Ishbaal is simply too weak; he is not the leader the nation needs.

My own heart is involved in this too, I know, because his refusal to let us marry was what made me finally realize his spitefulness and narrowness. But I have also known for some time that the nation's interests are not being well served by Ishbaal.

I do not know what my place will be in this new regime we are putting together. David has demands that will be met. But we did not discuss my role in his new kingdom. I know Joab and I will not easily serve together, even for this king. But I must trust David to work that out. Surely he can make Joab see the political reality of the situation and control him. I am somewhat relieved that even in this one face-to-face meeting I have come to feel that I can trust David to deal with this. I believe he will be a good king and look forward to serving him.

But above all else, I look forward to being with you soon.

Yours,
Abner

2.07 Joab Kills Abner
Joab (at Hebron) writes to his mother, Zeruiah (at Bethlehem)

Dearest Mother,
Abner is dead, and at my hand, as I promised you.

He came early this morning to Hebron to continue negotiations with David concerning establishing him as king of all Israel. I had been away for three days leading a raid (a most successful one!) and did not see him. I expect David arranged to have me gone during Abner's visit. But the city was full of talk about it when I got back, as he had only just departed.

I went to David and protested. I tried again, as before, to convince him that Abner is untrustworthy and that this was a chance to deal with Abner once and for all. David would not listen. The throne of Israel and his supposed "promise from the Lord" to sit upon it mean more to him than does the blood of Asahel. But not to me! Since he would do nothing himself, I sent word in David's name to bring Abner back, but did not tell David of it.

Abner had not gone far and soon returned with my messenger. I met him outside the gate and asked for a private conversation with him before he saw the king again. I know he has avoided me since Asahel's death, but the fool thought he was safe. After all, he had apparently been summoned back to court by David, and he suspected nothing.

And there outside the wall I killed him. It is justice. He stabbed Asahel, and I stabbed him. Let him burn in sheol. Abishai was with me, but it was my hand that did it.

We are avenged for Asahel, Mother, as I promised.

David was angry, or at least he made himself appear to be so before the people. Can he *really* be unhappy to have the one who is effectively king of Israel removed? But he appeared angry. He ordered me and the host to lead the procession of mourning for Abner, and he himself walked in the place of chief mourner behind the bier. He buried Abner in the city itself. The rebel should have been thrown on the refuse fires!

David sang another of his songs of lament, and the people all were pleased with him for weeping over this death. He can do no wrong in their eyes, Mother! Even the things that are foolish seem attractive to them. He blamed me openly for this – our family, really, "the sons of Zeruiah," so your name was mentioned too.

But apart from his harsh words about us, there has been no punishment, and it is clear that there will be none. Perhaps he realizes, as we have done for some time, that Abner needed to be removed. Perhaps all of his mourning and his disowning the deed are just wisdom. The people of Judah *and* the people of Israel want a king who will not take his kingdom by force but only at the apparent will of the people. So he seems content to have the kingdom, and even accepts the bloodshed so long as others cause it. Sometimes he seems so weak! Yet we know the people love him.

I have had vengeance. And the price I have paid is only a curse from the king and a minor humiliation. This is a day in which to rejoice, Mother. Vengeance cannot bring Asahel back, but it can salve the wound a little.

Your loving son,
Joab

2.08 David's Meditation: Lament for Abner
David writes at Hebron

> Should Abner die as a fool dies?
> Your hands were not bound,
> > your feet were not fettered;
> as one falls before the wicked
> > you have fallen.

2.09 Assassination of Ishbaal
Abigail (at Hebron) writes to her sister Sarah (at Bethel)

Dear sister,
Of course I'll come for your daughter's wedding. But David will not be with me. The affairs of the kingdom are particularly pressing now.

This long war with the house of Saul is over, and he is about to become king of all Israel and Judah. He has been fighting Ishbaal in a way that he would not have fought Saul. Rather, he's been fighting Abner, because Ishbaal is nothing.

With the death of Abner (which you will have heard of) David has hurried to conclude his negotiations with the elders of Israel. He wants to take advantage of the fear induced in the people (and in Ishbaal himself, we heard) by Abner's loss. What looked like a real disaster for David – the death of the one who was working to make him king – has turned to his advantage. These negotiations have been going on for the week since Abner was killed, but a new development has made them even more urgent.

Ishbaal himself has been killed. You will not likely have heard of this yet, though the news will spread quickly through the land. We have just heard of it here.

Two of Ishbaal's own raiders killed him. Baanah ben-Rimmon and his brother Rechab, of the tribe of Benjamin, known to us by reputation for their tactics and successes, were the assassins. They went into Ishbaal's house on the pretence of obtaining supplies and murdered him in his bed.

They then came to Hebron, bringing Ishbaal's head to David. They claimed that their work was the work of God in avenging David for the wrong that Saul had done in attempting to kill

David. I heard some of the old soldiers saying it reminded them of David's own carrying of another bloody head into the presence of a king, when he spoke with Saul after killing the giant Goliath.

David was in a rage at this. He recalled his treatment of the messenger who told him Saul was dead. He invoked the name of God himself, declared Ishbaal an innocent man wickedly murdered, and had these brothers killed. And then the head of Ishbaal received better treatment than Goliath's must have: David had Ishbaal's head buried in the tomb he made for Abner within the walls of this city. He has treated both Abner and Ishbaal like heroes and kings.

I wish I knew more of what he really thinks, Sarah. He is known by all the people to be a brilliant planner, a person who keeps his thoughts to himself until he chooses to reveal what his plans have accomplished. This is truer than the people know. It angers and frustrates me that it is also true within his family. I could gladly listen to his plans, and even help him to develop them. I am a woman who ran a large and complex estate on my own; Nabal, the drunken fool, was of no value in that as in other aspects of our marriage. All this before I married David, while he was still an outlaw in the wilderness, not yet subtle in the ways of statecraft. He knew this about me when he married me. Why does he continue to shut me out?

This is a tense time in the kingdom. His negotiations with the elders are so close to completion that he does not want the complication of this death of Ishbaal. He did not need to have Saul's son killed, because the elders were almost ready to remove the kingship from him. He certainly does not want the implication that God ordained this death on his behalf, or even a hint that David might have arranged it on his own behalf! He must denounce it so that he can remain an acceptable king for Israel.

But I sometimes wonder what he really believes when he invokes the name of God. So many circumstances seem to work out to David's advantage. Is this because God is indeed working on his behalf? Or is he able to see the advantage for himself in everything?

When I married him, I had recognized his intelligence and his subtlety. The way he dealt with the unlikely collection of misfits I first saw him with in the desert, and the way he evaded Saul (who had a much larger force and all the obvious advantages) –

these were evidence to me that he was an unusually intelligent leader. When I went to his camp to head off his planned attack against Nabal, I was impressed with how he responded to my arguments and to me. I had never been drawn to any man with that powerful combination of physical desire and admiration of who he was, or could become, because of how he thought and behaved. I had hoped that I might be one of his counsellors, that I might be included in his plans. I would have found that a fulfilling role. But I share only his bed, not his mind. It's not what I expected, as I have told you so often over the years.

This is rambling, and I beg your forgiveness. I will come in two days to help you prepare for the wedding. David will send a gift, but he will be occupied with the affairs of the kingdom. I will bring Chileab with me, and one of the servants to look after him. I want you to see how he has grown.

With love,
Abigail

2.10 Rizpah Mourns Abner's Death
Rizpah (at Gibeah) writes to Marah, Saul's niece (at Gibeah)

Marah,
By the time you find this note I'll be gone from Gibeah. While we've not been close, I know that many people talk to you. I want to leave word with someone, so I chose you.

Your uncle, Saul, took me from my home to be part of his harem. I was nothing to him but a symbol of the control he had over our village. My life here in his capital was empty and lonely. All of his women kept to themselves because no one in that household could understand your uncle or what he would do next. And no other person could be trusted. I was not sorry when he died in battle.

Under the new regime with Ishbaal as king I was able to enjoy a bit more freedom. When Abner and I came together, I thought life had begun at last. Now he's dead from this cursed war too! Your family and its intrigues are more than I can bear. I'm leaving tonight before anyone thinks of handing me over to some other man. I'll go back to my family in Gezer. If I'm ever needed, look for me there. I hope nobody ever looks.

Rizpah

2.11 David, King of Israel
Abigail (at Hebron) writes to her sister Sarah (at Bethel)

Dear Sarah,
He has it at last. He has learned patience since those days when he was in the desert. He would not wait to move against Nabal, but he has waited seven years to have Ishbaal gone so he could be king of all Israel.

Those desert days seem so long ago and so uncomplicated when I look back on them. David had the care of only a few hundred men then and had time for his family. As king of Judah he has been more and more occupied and away from us. I will say it: away from me.

Now that he is king of all Israel, his attention will turn even more to the realm and public things. I almost don't know who he is in private any more. He still writes and sings his songs, but he does not tell any of us how he thinks about them, or where in his experience they come from.

But he does tell some things. The story of Samuel anointing him when he was a young shepherd in Bethlehem, *that* story he tells. At least, he has told it in the past. He has not needed to tell it himself for a long time. It has been the basis of Judah's hope of ascendancy among the tribes, the source from which Judahites have drawn their patience for so long. So they have told the story. Perhaps it is even the source from which David has drawn his own hope and patience.

The elders of Israel have heard the story too and referred to it when they came to him. It was inevitable that they would come. Their government is in chaos, and they need a king to bring them order. Abner was the real power, and when he decided to come over to David, the end was in sight. Today they came to Hebron to make David their king. The negotiations that Abner began were easily completed.

But, as I said, the talk in public was not of kingdoms, war, generals, and murdered kings. In front of the people all the words were about the Lord's promise to David that he would rule in Israel.

So this is the beginning of the reign of the shepherd king, as he will style himself. He practised in Judah and is ready to rule all Israel. I believe he will be a good king, maybe even be a great king. He has a way of making people, even his adversaries, admire him and respect what he says and does. He can appear to be so guileless that people are immediately drawn to him. I myself felt this when I first met him in the desert. And I believe that Abner felt it for years but resisted falling under David's influence out of loyalty to Saul, until Ishbaal acted like a fool. Then Abner saw David's guilelessness as something to be valued in Israel's king.

And David can be a giving person. He understands love, how to evoke it and how to respond to it, how to nurture it. This will make him a good king. What could make him great is his amazing ability to come through trouble unharmed. We've spoken of it often. He says the experience is like going through a valley with a great shadow hanging over it, and being able to find his way to the other end. He says the shadow is dark, and feels like the approach of death. If he can do this for Israel as he has done it for himself, he could be a great king. The Lord knows that there certainly are valleys ahead: the Philistines, unifying the tribes into one nation, stabilizing trade inside and with our neighbours.

But I fear, sister, that though David will be a king to remember, he will not be the husband I had hoped for. I am part of a large household here, just one of many. There is only a king; there is no queen in David's kingdom. And he seems to have little thought of any of his wives in his mind, except at night!

The Lord is with him. He says it, Judah has said it for the past seven years, and now the elders of Israel have said it. Because of this, they have made him king. The Lord has made him king; they have only done what the Lord wanted. I don't know why the Lord has brought me into this, though.

But enough. I want to hear of you and your family. It has been too long since your last letter. As you can tell from what I write, I am lonely, and I long to have word from you. I'm not sure, though, where to tell you I will be. There is talk that we must move again. Hebron has been a good city from which to rule Judah, but a king of Israel must not show excessive loyalty to his own tribe. I don't know how David will handle this, but I expect he will take us somewhere else. It would be a slight to Saul's people to take over his capital in Gibeah, so it will have to be some new place. Write to me here: if we are gone, some of David's staff will be left behind and will find me with your letter.

With love and haste,
Abigail

2.12 David Chooses His Capital
Abigail (at Jerusalem) writes to her sister Sarah (at Bethel)

Dear Sarah,
Now that I know where we'll be, I'm writing to let you know and still hope that you will come. We're living in Jerusalem. Can you believe it?

After all these years of having that city unconquered in the middle of the tribes of Israel, David has taken it. I think he wanted some place that is central to the nation. He also wanted a place that did not either stress or deny his origin in Judah – thus whether he would be in a Judahite city or a non-Judahite city elsewhere in Israel was tricky business. And he wanted a place that would be *his* city. In fact, the part of the city into which we've moved is already being called "the city of David."

He certainly did not choose Jerusalem because it was easy to conquer. The Jebusites were so confident of their fortifications that with the city shut up they were sure nobody could get in. They taunted David, saying that even the blind and lame could defend the city against him.

My husband is nothing if not a good warrior and leader, though. He agreed that the city walls would be difficult to attack. But he told his men that since there is no well in Jerusalem, there had to be a way to bring in water from outside the walls. Whoever led the attack through the water shaft up into the fortified area, he declared, would be his commander-in-chief. His nephew Joab has been doing this job already and did not want to be displaced, so it was he who led the first approach.

Once inside, there was no stopping them. The Jebusites did not expect them to get in at all, and certainly did not expect such a surprise as to have warriors come through the water shaft. It was as though *they* were blind and lame.

David plans to reign from here. This will be popular, I think, because this conquered city represents the new king's might and nothing of the old ways in Israel or in Judah. Joab, who led the attack, is becoming increasingly important to David, and will surely have a large role in the kingdom David will now build. I'm disappointed to say that I expect no role for myself, even though I believe I could help him more than most of those around him.

So we will be here for a long time. Come to me in Jerusalem, dear sister.

Love,
Abigail

2.13 Retrieving the Ark
Obed-edom (at Kidon) to his friend Jehoshuah (at Kiriath Jearim)

My friend,
I've received a terrifying gift.

You've probably heard of the idea of the new king, David, to bring to the new capital the ancient Ark that is called by the Name of God. Moses had that old Ark made in the wilderness to carry the sacred objects. The Philistines captured it from us before David was born. It was returned to our people after the punishment of our God fell on the Philistines but was given no real importance when Samuel was judge or Saul was king.

Everyone in this part of the country knew about King David's idea, so you may already have heard of it. He had consulted widely to get support for what he intended to do. He has said that if the people of Israel and the God of Israel were in favour of it, he would bring the Ark to the king's city. And of course there was much support for it.

It's good to have a king who wants to consult with the people. It's good to have a king who wants to build new patterns of royal behaviour on old ones. It's good, at least for many of us, to have a king who openly worships the Lord, the God of our fathers.

It all started well. There were crowds, there was singing, there was dancing. The Ark was put on a cart guided by David's followers, including Uzzah, at the house of Abinadab in Kiriath Jearim. The procession moved without incident to our town of Kidon. Here the oxen stumbled. Uzzah seemed to think that the Ark was going to fall and reached out to steady it. Even in such a case, though, our God does not tolerate any setting aside of his laws and practices. Uzzah should not have touched the Ark because this is a privilege reserved for those who serve in the traditional way of the Levites. Uzzah died on the spot. May he rest with the Lord.

Perhaps there was some presumptuousness in it. Those who knew Uzzah well, as I did not, said he had a large sense of his own importance. Perhaps he would not wait for someone else, a Levite, to save the Ark.

King David had been strongly convinced that God was with him in this. But when Uzzah died, he questioned whether God really wanted this bringing of the Ark to the king's city. He was so agitated that none of his advisors dared face him or question what he was doing.

The procession was near my house when this incident occurred. David asked what was close by, and when he was given my name, sent the Ark to me to keep. He did not ask if I wanted it! This is an awesome honour. The Ark is holy. Evidently the God of our fathers still cares about it. Pray for me that I will treat it with the respect it deserves so that no harm comes to me or my family because of it.

I love the Lord, but I also fear him.

Under the mercy,
Obed-edom

2.14 David Is Victorious over the Philistines
Abishai (at Jerusalem) writes to his mother, Zeruiah (at Bethlehem)

Dear Mother,
The Lord has shown that he is present with the king. At least, that is what David claims has happened.

The Philistines, having heard that Israel had made David king, came to find him. But rather than waiting for them, my lord took the battle to them. They came against us through one of the valleys leading inland, and there on two occasions we defeated them.

In the first battle God told the king to attack directly, and the enemy were defeated easily. David named the place of the battle Baal Perizim, "The Lord Who Breaks Out," because he said that the Lord had broken out against his enemies just as water breaks out from a dam or a jug. As they fled, the enemy soldiers left their idols, and all our soldiers burned them to show the greatness of the Lord.

Then the Philistines returned a second time, and David again inquired of the Lord whether he should go to battle against them. In this second battle he was told to come from behind and to attack when he heard a sound of marching in the trees. This sound was to be a sign from the Lord that symbolized the marching of the Lord to lead us into battle, David said. Again we were successful and drove our enemies from Gibeah to Gezer.

David presents himself as the king whom the Lord leads into battle. These battles were an important test. David needed to show our enemies that he could command in all Israel, and he needed to show Israel that he could defeat our enemies when the people followed him. All nations are learning that he is a leader to fear and to respect and that this nation is a mighty nation. It is good to be part of what is happening here.

With love,
Abishai

2.15 Installing the Ark in Jerusalem
Michal (at Jerusalem) writes to her cousin Marah (at Gibeah)

Dear cousin,
We had a great festival here yesterday. I told you how disappointed David was three months ago that he had left the Ark of the Covenant partway along its journey to his new capital. In the meantime the place where he wanted to put it has remained empty. While he has been embarrassed before the entire nation by that emptiness, the household of Obed-edom, who has kept the Ark for David, has been prospering, and this has been widely known.

So David made great plans to fetch the Ark and bring it the remainder of the way to Jerusalem. In his usual way, he made a great occasion of it. He had arranged for a large number of musicians and singers to accompany the Ark on its journey.

He made sacrifices to the Lord for the success of the journey (this, of course, to avoid the horror of the previous attempt). The elders of the people as well as his officials and military leaders all were with him in the group that walked with the Ark.

You can imagine it: the music, the singing, the official party, the religious leaders carrying the Ark. The entire event was surrounded with a formal reverence for the Ark and for the Lord who has already demonstrated a willingness to act if the appropriate respect is not shown. At the same time there was a great celebration led by the musicians. It drew a large crowd of the common people. They always want to be near "their king," and he had provided them with a spectacle well worth seeing.

But David cannot seem to behave as a king should behave. No one responded with more energy to the music than he did. He sang loudly. The crowd was dancing – and so was David! I did not see them until they were close to the city. By then I believed the occasion had lost any sense of decorum or dignity.

Everyone was cheering and singing and dancing. David was in the centre of it all, close to the Ark and the focus of all attention. He danced wildly, without reserve. He did not dampen their fervour but rather fuelled it. The common people, including slave girls, surrounded him. And he was whirling and jumping so that his robe was no cover to him at all and he was almost naked!

I was embarrassed, but for him it was a great success. The Ark is now here with him so he can tell his people that the Lord stands behind his kingship. His plans have been accomplished, and no trace of the shame associated with his earlier attempt remains. He had a good party and received great adulation from the people. He established a new place and pattern of worship in the heart of his new capital.

When the Ark was finally placed where it will remain, he gave everyone gifts of food, and they were all pleased with him and with the day's events. Yet I can't see what is so worthy of attention here. I've heard the old stories, but this is not the usual business of a king. It's an old box – yes, it's beautifully made – and it has contained old relics of a past time. Surely David must mean to make more of this to have it be worth the trouble he's gone to. But he does not talk of this to me. He barely talks to me at all.

So I spoke to him afterwards about the day and his behaviour. I told him my concern is for the dignity of this house. What I did not say is that my passion is for David. But his passion is not for me – it is for his God and for these curious ways in which he feels he needs to express his devotion. And that passion causes him to act without the restraint that dignity requires. My father was not as popular a king as is David, but he at least knew the proper way for a king and a king's family to behave.

David was not pleased with me. He made no apology for his actions and even justified them to me. He has no shame before the people. He has more intimacy with the Lord and the people of Israel than with me. He and I are growing further apart. Why has this happened? I have loved this man for so long. I said so before we were married, and that prompted my father to offer me to him. But what has he given to me? Our first time together was too short for anything other than the excitement of coming to know each other's bodies. Before we could make a life or a family, David fled from my father. And my father never cared about me, I learned then. He gave me to another man, even though I still longed for David. When David did return after my father's death, he only wanted me as a symbol. Has he ever loved me? Where is his devotion to God in this? I have suffered for nothing other than loving him. God loves, David says. Can David not love me? I hoped that what I said to him today would bring him to his senses and bring him closer to me, but I fear it has not.

I long for your next letter, and for your next visit.

Love,
Michal

2.16 Michal Is Barren
Michal (at Jerusalem) writes to her cousin Marah (at Gibeah)

Dear cousin,
We are both now old women. I had not expected to live this long. I had certainly not expected as a child in Saul's court that I would see all that I have seen as David's wife. I do not think that I have much time left in this world. I cannot travel to see you, and I know you are not able to come to me.

But I want to tell you something I've hidden even from you, the one who knows my secrets and sorrows. It is no secret that the king and I have had a strained relationship for many years. And you know that we have had no children, though David has many children from his other wives. What you do not know is that David has not shared my bed for most of our married life.

When I returned to him from Paltiel, we came together each with quite different expectations. The marriage was uncomfortable for us both. The final breakdown occurred when I chastized him over his actions when the Ark was brought to the city. I mocked him for his behaviour with the slave girls. I wanted him to be more restrained and regal, and he was angered by my words.

Because of that, I have no children. I have not even had a husband except in name.

I loved him in the early years and when I came back to him. But rejection has made me hate him. I was his first wife and the daughter of a king. I should have been his queen. But David has made no wife queen.

So devoted is he to his work and his dreams for the nation, and so devoted to the Lord as he understands the Lord, that everything and everyone else gets set aside.

I know you have felt sorrow at my barrenness. I have not been able to tell even you that it had such a simple cause. Death will be release from an empty life.

Love,
Michal

2.17 David's Meditation: Installation of the Ark
David writes at Jerusalem

> O give thanks to the Lord, call on his name,
> > make known his deeds among the peoples.
> Sing to him, sing praises to him,
> > tell of all his wonderful works.
> Glory in his holy name;
> > let the hearts of those who seek the Lord rejoice.
> Seek the Lord and his strength,
> > seek his presence continually.
> Remember the wonderful works he has done,
> > his miracles, and the judgments he uttered,

O offspring of his servant Israel,
   children of Jacob, his chosen ones.

He is the Lord our God;
   his judgments are in all the earth.
Remember his covenant forever,
   the word that he commanded, for a thousand generations,
the covenant that he made with Abraham,
   his sworn promise to Isaac,
which he confirmed to Jacob as a statute,
   to Israel as an everlasting covenant,
saying, "To you I will give the land of Canaan
   as your portion for an inheritance."

When they were few in number,
   of little account, and strangers in the land,
wandering from nation to nation,
   from one kingdom to another people,
he allowed no one to oppress them;
   he rebuked kings on their account,
saying, "Do not touch my anointed ones;
   do my prophets no harm."

Sing to the Lord, all the earth.
   Tell of his salvation from day to day.
Declare his glory among the nations,
   his marvelous works among all the peoples.
For great is the Lord, and greatly to be praised;
   he is to be revered above all gods.
For all the gods of the peoples are idols,
   but the Lord made the heavens.
Honor and majesty are before him;
   strength and joy are in his place.

Ascribe to the Lord, O families of the peoples,
   ascribe to the Lord glory and strength.
Ascribe to the Lord the glory due his name;
   bring an offering, and come before him.
Worship the Lord in holy splendor;
   tremble before him, all the earth.

The world is firmly established; it shall never be moved.
Let the heavens be glad, and let the earth rejoice,
   and let them say among the nations, "The Lord is king!"
Let the sea roar, and all that fills it;
   let the field exult, and everything in it.
Then shall the trees of the forest sing for joy
   before the Lord, for he comes to judge the earth.
O give thanks to the Lord, for he is good;
   for his steadfast love endures forever.

Say also: "Save us, O God of our salvation,
   and gather and rescue us from among the nations,
that we may give thanks to your holy name,
   and glory in your praise.
Blessed be the Lord, the God of Israel,
   from everlasting to everlasting."

2.18 God Establishes David's Reign
Nathan the prophet (at Jerusalem) writes to Gad the prophet (at Jericho)

Dear colleague,
I look forward to your returning soon and an opportunity to talk together, as we have so often done before, and to seek your consolation. Even in old age I have not learned to speak only after careful consideration.

King David spoke to me yesterday of his desire to build a temple to the Lord. He now has the Ark in Jerusalem, but only in a tent. He wanted, he said, to honour the Lord by replacing the tent with a temple. No doubt he also wants to establish his capital city more firmly in the minds of the people of Israel.

The king is clearly favoured of the Lord. His reign over Judah and his ascendancy now over Israel are evidence of that, as is his success in completing the journey of the Ark. It certainly seemed to me consistent with all that has transpired to develop a national centre of worship here, focused on a temple. And so I told the king.

But afterwards in the night the word of the Lord God came to me unsought. And not only was the coming of the word unanticipated but I was surprised by what he said to me. There is to be a temple, but David is not to build it. Instead, the Lord's supremacy over this kingdom is to be seen in a different way. The Ark is to remain in the tent. But David will be the first king in a dynasty, and his son will build the temple of the Lord. So David wanted to establish the Lord's house, but instead the Lord will establish David's house.

I was distressed and fearful as I went to the king today to tell him of this message. But just as with the Lord, so with David: he can always surprise me. He was not angry but instead went to pray alone. I almost wondered if he had expected a different answer than the one I gave too quickly yesterday.

I serve two masters, God and King David. It is easy to want to please the king, and to speak for God in such a way that God's words convey what I think David wants. But this serves neither master well and jeopardizes my own position. David wants truth and always accepts it, frequently even thanking me for it. God will allow nothing else.

I send this so you know what to expect when you get here.

Under the mercy,
Nathan

2.19 David's Meditation: Prayer for the Dynasty
David writes at Jerusalem

Who am I, O Lord God, and what is my house, that you have brought me thus far? And yet this was a small thing in your eyes, O Lord God; you have spoken also of your servant's house for a great while to come. May this be instruction for the people, O Lord God!

And what more can David say to you? For you know your servant, O Lord God! Because of your promise, and according to your own heart, you have wrought all this greatness, so that your servant may know it.

Therefore you are great, O Lord God; for there is no one like you, and there is no God besides you, according to all that we have heard with our ears. Who is like your people, like Israel? Is there another nation on earth whose God went to redeem it as a people, and to make a name for himself, doing great and awesome things for them, by driving out before his people nations and their gods? And you established your people Israel for yourself to be your people forever; and you, O Lord, became their God.

And now, O Lord God, as for the word that you have spoken concerning your servant and concerning his house, confirm it forever; do as you have promised. Thus your name will be magnified forever in the saying, "The Lord of hosts is God over Israel"; and the house of your servant David will be established before you.

For you, O Lord of hosts, the God of Israel, have made this revelation to your servant, saying, "I will build you a house"; therefore your servant has found courage to pray this prayer to you. And now, O Lord God, you are God, and your words are true, and you have promised this good thing to your servant; now therefore may it please you to bless the house of your servant, so that it may continue forever before you; for you, O Lord God, have spoken, and with your blessing shall the house of your servant be blessed forever.

3 Reign

Zadok the Scribe's Commentary

Bloodshed and suffering, as we have seen in the previous group of documents, followed David and those around him all his life. Is this necessary for a king, and especially for one who claims to be God's king? For example, what Michal reveals about her barrenness is hard to reconcile with the idea of David that I had before reading these letters. How could he make someone endure such suffering for so long? Did he believe that serving God as king required him to treat Michal this way? Certainly those around him did not fully understand him.

This next group of documents relates to a new phase in David's life. When David assumed the throne of the unified nation, he set about establishing his own pattern of rule. He was successful in early battles against the nation's enemies. He put together a council of advisors that included some of the wisest people in the nation. He reached out to the household of Saul, through the son of his own friend, Prince Jonathan.

Unfortunately what began well did not continue well. David's reign was plagued by problems. Some he created for himself, and others seemed to emerge from those difficulties. He committed adultery with the wife of one of the heroes of his army, and to cover it up, murdered her husband. This seems to have weakened him to the extent that he was unable to deal with other issues.

He did not control his own children. One son, Amnon, raped one of David's daughters, his half-sister Tamar. Another son, Absalom, killed Amnon to avenge the rape. Civil war in Israel resulted when the turmoil within the family spilled over into the nation's affairs, with Absalom leading the revolt.

David was forced to flee into the desert to escape his own son. This period in his life is reminiscent in many ways of his earlier periods in the desert both as a shepherd and while fleeing from Saul. In this later period, though, David is not the dashing hero that he was in the earlier stories. He survives now through cunning and some key battles. The civil disturbance is resolved when Absalom dies at Joab's hand, in spite of David's command that his son not be harmed.

Clearly these events affected David deeply. But the documents written by those around him do not interpret his actions in the same terms as in the earlier part of his life. The faith David had in God is not expressed in the same confident manner as before. His request for God's forgiveness after the adultery and murder is poignant, but however he understood the response from God, he was unable to regain his former dynamic leadership. Even so, he apparently continued to command the loyalty and respect of many leaders in the nation and of the people as a whole.

The writers of these documents are from David's immediate family (especially his wives, for whom the adultery was surely a critical issue), and from those close to him in the royal court in the army and in religious offices.

The events of this period are key to understanding David as an individual, but they are difficult to reconcile with the stature he attained in the intervening years. Kings of Israel and Judah are regularly assessed in our ancient writings by the standard set by David — not the standard of David evident in this part of his life, the man who sins, who commits adultery and murder, who is unable to retain leadership in his family or in the nation, but the standard of a man who is fully committed to God.

These documents continue to demonstrate that David was complex. They also continue to demonstrate that the portrait of David in our sacred texts is sparse and terse, leaving out much of what he and the people around him thought about the events taking place around them.

3.01 David's Initial Victories in Battle

Ahinoam (at Jerusalem) writes to her sister Milcah (at Jezreel)

My dearest sister,
Life in the new capital is strange for me. I miss you and the rest of the family and wish that you could visit more often. I'm mostly

occupied with life in the palace and my place as the mother of the king's first-born son.

The household is large and complicated. In part the complications come from the relationships among us, David's wives. Michal was his first wife, but they now have nothing to do with each other, and she is a difficulty in anything that needs to be done. David does not speak to her, and the rest of us avoid her sarcasm as much as we can. Whatever there might have been between her and David in the past is gone on both sides.

Abigail is the strongest personality among us and is quite ready to make plans and arrangements. But because she did not give David his first son, she does not have the place of authority that falls to me. I'd rather she had it than I! Running a large house and family in such a public setting is not what I wanted from life.

Even David is not much comfort. He is always occupied with the kingship and often away. Even though there are many here who are devoted to him and thus eager to help in the household affairs, it is not the same as when we were together in the early days.

Much of his time has been spent in fighting on the borders of Israel, pushing back our enemies and enlarging our own territory and wealth. I'm sure you'll have heard of these campaigns. For David and for Israel they mean prestige and wealth, but for me they mean frequent absences by my husband and danger for him when he is fighting.

He believes that the Philistines have been driven out of our land for good in the west, which is a welcome relief to all our people. But he has also extended the kingdom to the east in Moab, to the northeast in Zobah, to the north in Hamath, and to the south in Edom. Our enemies must be in awe of us now, because there have been many battles and David has almost always been victorious.

The nation of Israel is now really an empire because David rules lands not traditionally ours and people who are not part of our own twelve tribes. He claims to do this for God and to bring back the wealth and the tribute from these defeated enemies to devote them to the glory of God. I'm pleased that he's successful. And I am successful too, I suppose, beyond what I expected as a girl. But this success has its price.

So all this is to excuse myself once again from attending the family gathering this year. It's not that I won't admit my birth, as some of our cousins say, but simply that I am too occupied here to get away.

I would love to see you, though, if you can come to me again after the harvest is complete. Bring your children if they can be spared from the work of the farm. Give my love to all our family when you are together.

Love,
Ahinoam

3.02 David's Meditation: Celebration of Victory
David writes at Jerusalem

> O God, you have rejected us, broken our defenses;
>   you have been angry; now restore us!
> You have caused the land to quake; you have torn it open;
>   repair the cracks in it, for it is tottering.
> You have made your people suffer hard things;
>   you have given us wine to drink that made us reel.
>
> You have set up a banner for those who fear you,
>   to rally to it out of bowshot.
>
> Give victory with your right hand, and answer us,
>   so that those whom you love may be rescued.
>
> God has promised in his sanctuary:
>   "With exultation I will divide up Shechem,
>   and portion out the Vale of Succoth.
> Gilead is mine, and Manasseh is mine;
>   Ephraim is my helmet;
>   Judah is my scepter.
> Moab is my washbasin;
>   on Edom I hurl my shoe;
>   over Philistia I shout in triumph."
>
> Who will bring me to the fortified city?
>   Who will lead me to Edom?
> Have you not rejected us, O God?

> You do not go out, O God, with our armies.
> O grant us help against the foe,
>   for human help is worthless.
> With God we shall do valiantly;
>   it is he who will tread down our foes.

3.03 David Establishes a Government
Abishai (at Jerusalem) writes to his mother, Zeruiah (at Bethlehem)

Dear Mother,

I have very good news for you about Joab. Nothing you won't have expected, but it's good to have it confirmed all the same. You will have been watching from where you are the same pattern I have been seeing from much closer.

The king has established a stable government in Israel. At first it was important to gain the support of the people. He did that through very skilful negotiations leading up to his being crowned king of Judah and then king of Israel.

Then he needed to stabilize the extent of the country (or perhaps I should say empire) and establish understandings with the surrounding nations. This has been largely accomplished. Not only do we have more land and more wealth than Israel has ever had but we may even be heading into a time of peace.

This nation is much larger than the band of men David led years ago in the desert, where he could make all decisions himself. A country needs ministers, a cabinet, and established areas of responsibility. David has thus needed to establish an administration.

So I am very pleased that David has confirmed again that my brother Joab will lead the army. This is a controversial appointment, because not all the people are comfortable with Joab. He certainly has skill as a warrior and as a general, but you know that he is not easily liked as a person. The people believe him to be capable of great cruelty. Even other close advisors to David are concerned about Joab's brashness in dealing with the king and in reprimanding him. But David has decided, and he will need to live with the consequences of this decision.

Joab is the only one from our family who is to have a major role, it seems. I know David still talks about us and distrusts our strong responses. But I'm content to see Joab recognized and to help when he asks. I don't want the burden of leadership myself.

Other responsibilities have been allocated to others here in the palace and in the capital. David may establish a pattern of rule that other kings will follow, and we may put in place ways of running the country that will last for a long time to come.

With love,
Abishai

3.04 David and Mephibosheth
Abigail (at Jerusalem) writes to her sister Sarah (at Bethel)

Dear Sarah,

I'm weary from the worries about danger for so many years and from the many changes in our lives recently. But perhaps things are becoming calmer at last. The patterns of life in this new kingdom are starting to become evident.

In the early days after David was crowned, the sense of excitement and anticipation was tremendous. Of course, there were those who had supported the house of Saul and were thus very disappointed. Others among the twelve tribes of Israel wanted to diminish what David had done and argued that he was not suited to rule the nation. Those old tribal rivalries are often just under the surface in this country. But most people were willing to put them aside and look to the future. And the future was exciting, because it was unknown and because David seemed to embody so much promise.

Well, the nation is starting to see what kind of king they have chosen. David has been victorious in battle and has established the borders of a nation much larger than anyone had expected. He attributes all of this to God. Because there is peace, people are able to devote themselves to their farms and businesses, so there is prosperity. Of course, there is also prosperity because of what the king can afford to do! You would be astounded by the money and treasures that David has begun to amass and to use for building this nation. Much of it comes from tribute and wealth that he has taken from the nations around us as they have been defeated.

I know he plans to make this a beautiful capital city, but he has not spoken about the details of that dream. I hope to be part of the planning of all of that!

What you cannot know is what happens inside the palace, in the privacy of the household. Here too we are starting to see what kind of king David will be. To show you what I mean, I'll tell you one story.

You will remember that David was a very close friend to Jonathan, who might have been expected to become the next king after Saul. Jonathan's death at the side of his father fighting the enemies of Israel put an end to that hope. Since David has had some tranquility as his kingdom has become well established, he has begun to think back on his friendship with Jonathan. He asked if there was anyone remaining alive from Saul's household, intending to do something to honour that friendship.

As it turned out, Jonathan himself had a son named Mephibosheth. This young man was not killed in battle because he could not fight. His feet have been shrivelled from childhood when his nurse dropped him. He can only walk slowly and certainly cannot make a soldier, so when the rest of the family went to battle and died, he was left at home. When David was told about Mephibosheth, he was happy that it was Jonathan's own son who had been found. Mephibosheth came to the palace in fear, knowing that his grandfather's family still has supporters who worry David. But David made it clear he wished to fulfil a promise he had made to Jonathan, and that no harm would come to Mephibosheth.

David decided to give Mephibosheth all the land that had belonged to the house of Saul. Of course, Mephibosheth cannot work the land himself, so David commissioned Ziba, a servant of the house of Saul, to be a servant now of Mephibosheth and to work the land. The income from the estate will provide for Ziba and all his family, and also for Mephibosheth.

But beyond this, David has brought Mephibosheth into his own household. He lives in the palace and eats with our own family. David treats him as if he were his own son. It is almost as if he has adopted Mephibosheth. In fact, some say that in the son of Saul's son David sees the child that he would like to have fathered with Saul's daughter, Michal. If that other child had ever been born, he might have united the two dynasties of Saul and David in one. Because of the rift between David and Michal, that child will never be conceived. Some see Mephibosheth as representing a dream that for David has died.

But I see it quite differently. David does not dote on Mephibosheth. In fact, Mephibosheth is treated no differently from the others in the household. He is simply one of us. David seems to have moved on from his enthusiasm over his friendship with Jonathan. He has also set aside the accumulated grievances from the long war with Saul's household, and perhaps even the dream of uniting the two dynasties in one person. He decided to do a generous thing and he has done it, and he now acts as though there is nothing special about it.

That is what I wanted to tell you. From outside the palace the people of Israel see a king who is a great warrior. They see the public figure of a man growing into the responsibilities of his office. (This is something that Saul was never able to do. His reign was wild and uncertain at every point.) And the people see a man who gives credit to his God for all that he has accomplished. I see a man who is also able to move beyond the bad things in his life and to create good for himself and those around him.

Inside the palace we see something else as well. David remains a puzzle to me. All of us were surprised when he began to ask about Saul's household, and we were all surprised by his generosity to Mephibosheth. You can imagine the conflicts there are in such a large family, with so much at stake in being part of it. Some of David's sons (and their mothers) were not at all happy with Mephibosheth's arrival, and they let this be known. But now that it has been done, I begin to see it as part of the larger pattern of David's life. I wish that I were closer to him, as I have often told you. I had hoped that I would share his private thoughts, but he chooses not to share those with any of us.

And so I continue to value this exchange between us. I want to tell you about my life, and I am interested in yours and especially in how your children are developing. Please write to me soon.

Love,
Abigail

3.05 War with Ammon
Joab (at Jerusalem) writes to his mother, Zeruiah (at Bethlehem)

Dear Mother,
We are back, Abishai and I, from the battles against the Ammonites. It has been a glorious campaign, and you can be proud of what we both accomplished. David truly behaved like the king this nation needs! Our enemies have clearly seen the power of our army.

The conflict began unexpectedly, at least for me. A new king, Hanun, came to power in Ammon after the death of his father. Since David had established an allegiance with Ammon under the previous king, he sent envoys to greet the new king and to convey consolation about the old king's death. But Hanun and his advisors suspected the envoys of being sent to spy out the weaknesses of their kingdom and city and did not receive them. David's men were seized and mistreated. Each man had half his beard removed and his robes torn open up to the hips.

David was outraged at the behaviour of Hanun and the Ammonites, and immediately declared we would fight against them to avenge the wrong that had been done. But at the same time he sent a message to the envoys, telling them not to return to Jerusalem until their beards had grown back. He did not want them to be embarrassed in front of the court, the army, and the people. That he would think of these few and their standing in the community while in the midst of a national crisis is what makes the people love him.

Both of these aspects, though, relate to a dominant commitment in David. He treats promise and covenant as of utmost importance. Since there was a covenant between Israel and Ammon, he expected it to be fulfilled and was willing to fight when it was violated. Since he and his own men stand in a relationship of mutual promise and trust, he treats them with respect and concern.

Meanwhile, Hanun realized that David was angry and would reply with force. Perhaps the covenant that meant so much to David had had a more limited meaning to Ammon. Perhaps the previous king had seen David as a foil, a rival to Saul who would make Israel weak rather than strong, and the new king saw David as a threat now that he has gained so much power. In any case, Hanun augmented his own army with Aramean mercenaries.

David stayed in Jerusalem and I led the army to the battle. I split the company in two to face the two forces formed by Ammon on the one side and the Arameans on the other. Abishai and I each commanded a force, with the possibility that one might help the other, depending on how the battle went. But both enemy forces withdrew, the Ammonites back into their city, and the Arameans back to their own territory.

The Arameans were only regrouping, though, and gathering reinforcements, and were soon ready to fight on their own behalf. They too were fearful of Israel with a strong king. David himself came to lead the armies of Israel against the Arameans. It was a bloody fight with many soldiers and many leaders dead at the end of it, mostly on the Aramean side but some on ours as well. The defeated Arameans made peace with David and agreed to become his vassals.

The Ammonites have only run away, so we are not yet done with them, but the Arameans will not trouble us again.

David recognized Abishai and me as his most important generals. He let us fight, and he fought himself. This is the kind of leadership we have been looking for.

Your loving son,
Joab

3.06 The Death of Uriah
Joab (at Rabbah) writes to his mother, Zeruiah (at Bethlehem)

Dear Mother,
Here is a mystery for you. Perhaps you can find out from Jerusalem what is happening before I return home. I am now encamped with the army outside Rabbah, the capital city of Ammon. I am pursuing the campaign that was interrupted when David and I led the army against the Arameans, who had helped the Ammonites hold us back previously.

Last week I received a message from David asking for Uriah to be sent to him. Remember that Uriah was one of the heroes from the days when those of us with David were a small company wandering in the desert of Judah to escape King Saul. I didn't know what David's request meant, but of course I sent Uriah to him.

After only a couple of days in Jerusalem, Uriah returned carrying a letter from David. The letter instructed me to set Uriah in the forefront of the hardest fighting, and then draw back from him, so that he would be struck down. I would not have believed such an order conveyed to me indirectly, but this note was in David's own hand. So, as we next attacked the city, I put Uriah against the city wall where he was exposed to the defenders. As we were pulling back, a squad of Ammonites rushed out of the city. All of those Israelites closest to the wall, including Uriah, were killed.

I sent a messenger to David telling him of the battle plan and its results, clearly instructing the messenger to tell David of the death of Uriah. Now the messenger is back, but not with rebuke from David, as would normally be the case if I used such a foolish battle plan. Instead, he came with words of encouragement about the uncertainty of battle and the necessity to press the attack again tomorrow.

This is unusual. Something is happening that involved Uriah. I do not know what it is, but perhaps your informants can find out for you. Please write to me here because I am not sure how long it will take to defeat this city.

I have kept David's letter. I expect it could be extremely valuable to me.

Your loving son,
Joab

3.07 Why Uriah Died
Zeruiah (at Bethlehem) writes to her son Joab (at Rabbah)

My son,
I have solved the mystery you sent me, but be prepared for a shock. Our servants in the palace have communicated to me in confidence, but such a thing cannot be hidden for long. This will soon be common knowledge in the kingdom.

When you went to Rabbah to fight the Ammonites, David stayed in the palace. Did he give no indication of why he stayed behind? He should have been with you and this scandalous incident would not have happened.

Shortly after the army departed, from the palace walls David saw a beautiful woman bathing. He inquired who she was and learned that she was Bathsheba, the wife of Uriah.

David sent for her and slept with her. When she found that she was pregnant, she told David. He asked for Uriah to be sent home, obviously expecting that Uriah would also sleep with Bathsheba while in Jerusalem. His wife's child would then appear to be his, and the adultery would be hidden.

But this was not to be. David questioned Uriah about the battle and sent him away, expecting him to go home to Bathsheba. But Uriah was an unusual man, very dedicated to David and to the camaraderie of the army. He slept at the palace to be on hand if David wanted him again, treating his time in Jerusalem as if it were service in the army rather than a leave. After David tried for days to get Uriah to go home, he instead sent him back to you.

The instructions in the letter Uriah carried with him to you make David a murderer! You were right to keep it. It should protect you if he wants to move against you in future. Of course, you are also involved, but the greater fault is David's.

With Uriah dead, he has taken Bathsheba as one of his wives and moved her into the palace. These events may weaken his position with the people. Perhaps there is room now for a royal dynasty from the house of Jesse through our family rather than through David. Perhaps this failing on his part will give us something to exploit.

Press the battle. It would be good for you to overcome Rabbah quickly and return to Jerusalem to watch how this matter unfolds.

Lovingly,
Mother

3.08 Nathan Rebukes David

Nathan the prophet (at Jerusalem) writes to Gad the prophet (at Jericho)

Dear colleague,
Your responsibilities with our fellow prophets in Jericho often have you away when I need your advice. I look forward to a time when

they have sufficient leadership among themselves that you can stay here in the capital.

This has been a terrible day in Israel. Last night I had an oracle from the Lord unlike anything I had experienced. And today I carried out the commands of the Lord by speaking to King David.

The message that came to me last night was different from all others both in tone and content. The Lord communicated to me that he was angry, and this anger was something I had not previously known. The anger was directed at the king because of sin that he had committed.

I went to David this morning and told him a story. A poor man had a single lamb that he loved and looked after carefully. A rich man with large herds lived nearby. When a visitor came to the rich man's house, the rich man took the poor man's lamb to provide a feast.

David thought the story was true and became angry with the rich man. He said that the man would have to repay by four times what he had taken from the poor man. At that instant the power of the Lord came to me and I spoke without fear, pointing at David in front of his assembled court and saying, "You are the man!"

The Lord has blessed David, but David took what was not his from another man. He murdered Uriah, and he took Uriah's wife as his own.

Now the Lord has promised punishment for David. There will be fighting continually. There will be fighting within David's own family. His wives will be given to another man, not in secret, as David took Bathsheba, but in public.

I had gone with some fear into the king's presence, and when he became angry at the story of the lamb, my fear increased. But once the power of the Lord was upon me, I was not afraid. And when I finished speaking, David stood quietly for a moment, then said, "I have sinned against the Lord." This is the response that the Lord wanted, I believe. I do not know if I could have admitted before so many people what David admitted.

At that point the power of the Lord came upon me again. I told David that the Lord had accepted his confession and that he would not die. But the child of David and Bathsheba would die.

I hope never to face such a situation again. I have known that every person is imperfect, that every person sins before the Lord. But I, and many others, had hoped that David would be different.

I should learn from this not to put so much trust in any person, only in God.

Under the mercy,
Nathan

3.09 David and Bathsheba's Child Dies
Michal (at Jerusalem) writes to her cousin Marah (at Gibeah)

My cousin,
Perhaps news has not yet reached Gibeah of the trouble in this household. David has committed adultery with Bathsheba, the wife of one of his warriors, Uriah, resulting in a pregnancy. He continually ignores me, but he even stepped aside from the other wives to take this woman. He tried to have Uriah sent home from the wars on a pretence so that Uriah would sleep with Bathsheba and the child might be viewed as legitimate.

When that did not work, David had Uriah placed where he was sure to be killed in battle. Then David took the widowed Bathsheba as his own wife. But Nathan accused David before the entire court, and David confessed. This much is getting to be widely known, and even those who in the past disagreed with me can see he doesn't pay sufficient attention to what is required of a king!

What has happened today is that the child born to Bathsheba a week ago has died. Nathan warned that this would happen, but David has been fasting and praying all week, entreating God not to take the child – without success.

I have warned him repeatedly about his behaviour. He has been too close to the people. He has not shown the distance and decorum that the king must show. Now he has done something so common and low as to sleep with a soldier's wife and commit murder to cover it up.

The palace is in shock. David is in disgrace. There is no other person who could replace him as king, so he will surely continue, but his relationship with the court, with his family, and with the people of Israel will now be different. The hero who cannot fail is gone.

For me there is a certain bitter satisfaction in this. I have been disgraced by the treatment David has shown me, and now he has disgraced himself. Yet I find myself even more isolated. The rest of the household already did not accept me. Now they expect me to be pointing out the frailty of the great king, so they avoid me even more. I am lonely. There seems little to expect from the rest of my life. I long for your next visit.

With love,
Michal

3.10 David Reacts to the Death of His Child
Ahinoam (at Jerusalem) writes to her sister Milcah (at Jezreel)

Dear sister,
The child of David and Bathsheba has died. David was in agony during the week that the child lived but has once again surprised us by his reaction after the death.

His servants were afraid to tell him that the child had died because he had been so disturbed during the previous week. But David sensed that it had happened and asked them to confirm it, which they were forced to do. Instead of lamenting, he washed and changed and went to worship the Lord. When he came back his servants asked him about this behaviour which they did not understand.

He told them that while the child had lived, he had held out hope that the Lord would not carry through on the judgment that Nathan had pronounced on the child. (David loves to talk of the Lord's mercy, but in the end it was the Lord's righteousness, not his mercy, that was evident here: what God had said would result from David's sin in fact came to pass.) But with the child gone, there is now nothing to be done. David cannot bring him back. But he says he expects to "go to him" eventually – I suppose he means when he dies.

I have told you before that life near David has been full and rich. Now we are all watching an awful thing. He has been hurt before. He truly sorrowed over the deaths of Saul, Jonathan, and Abner and the danger to the nation when those deaths occurred. His laments then were painful to behold. But in all of that sorrow David was an observer. Now he is the cause. It is his actions with Bathsheba, with Uriah, and with Joab as his agent that have brought about this calamity. It is horrible to see how devastated he is by all of this, how much it has shaken his view of himself.

I do not know what the future holds for us now. David will continue as king. No one is of a mind to remove him. But a king who has committed adultery and murder will be thought of much differently by the people!

With love,
Ahinoam

3.11 The Birth of Solomon
Abigail (at Jerusalem) writes to her sister Sarah (at Bethel)

Dear sister,
There is another child in the family: David and Bathsheba have a son named Solomon.

Bathsheba continues as one of David's wives. Evidently he feels a particular commitment to her. I'm not sure it is love, although there may be some of that. I am sure that he feels that he has promised her something and so will fulfil his promise. He's committed to the notion of promise and covenant in his religious life, in his behaviour as king, and in his personal life. But I think there may be more between them that has not yet been told to the rest of us. David is so able to keep things to himself that we will certainly not learn unless he chooses to tell us.

Perhaps his commitment to Bathsheba was to give her a son after the death of their first child, conceived while she was married to Uriah. This baby's birth is a great comfort to Bathsheba. She has had a difficult time fitting into the household. On the one hand, she was involved in the scandal that has caused David to be seen as much less than what many had hoped him to be. On the other hand, she was clearly not the one who instigated the affair, nor was she an accomplice in the murder. But it has taken the rest of the family some time to be at ease with her. Now that she is a mother, it gives us all something to talk about and deal with more comfortably.

Even so, there is a great deal of anxiety in the palace. David is rebuilding the relationships he damaged when his adultery and murder were revealed last year. This will be a long and slow process. I don't believe that he can ever have the same authority that he had before. Yet he is a remarkable person and has a strong belief in the grace and mercy of God. He claims that for himself, and he expects others to behave as though God has granted it to him.

The prophet Nathan came to David to tell him that God has given the child the name Jedidiah, which means Beloved of the Lord. Perhaps this is a sign that God is as gracious to David as David claims him to be.

With love,
Abigail

3.12 David's Meditation: Confession
David writes at Jerusalem

> Have mercy on me, O God,
>   according to your steadfast love;
> according to your abundant mercy
>   blot out my transgressions.
> Wash me thoroughly from my iniquity,
>   and cleanse me from my sin.
> For I know my transgressions,
>   and my sin is ever before me.
> Against you, you alone, have I sinned,
>   and done what is evil in your sight,
> so that you are justified in your sentence
>   and blameless when you pass judgment.
> Indeed, I was born guilty,
>   a sinner when my mother conceived me.
>
> You desire truth in the inward being;
>   therefore teach me wisdom in my secret heart.
> Purge me with hyssop, and I shall be clean;
>   wash me, and I shall be whiter than snow.
> Let me hear joy and gladness;
>   let the bones that you have crushed rejoice.
> Hide your face from my sins,
>   and blot out all my iniquities.

Create in me a clean heart, O God,
    and put a new and right spirit within me.
Do not cast me away from your presence,
    and do not take your holy spirit from me.
Restore to me the joy of your salvation,
    and sustain in me a willing spirit.

Then I will teach transgressors your ways,
    and sinners will return to you.
Deliver me from bloodshed, O God,
    O God of my salvation,
    and my tongue will sing aloud of your deliverance.

O Lord, open my lips,
    and my mouth will declare your praise.
For you have no delight in sacrifice;
    if I were to give a burnt offering, you would not be pleased.
The sacrifice acceptable to God is a broken spirit;
    a broken and contrite heart, O God, you will not despise.

Do good to Zion in your good pleasure;
    rebuild the walls of Jerusalem,
then you will delight in right sacrifices,
    in burnt offerings and whole burnt offerings;
    then bulls will be offered on your altar.

3.13 The Capture of Rabbah
Joab (at Rabbah) writes to his mother, Zeruiah (at Bethlehem)

Dear Mother,

I will be leaving soon to return to Jerusalem. All that's left is to delegate the oversight of this city and arrange for the tribute.

    It is a week since I defeated the city after this long siege. I then sent for David so that he could be the one to enter the city and take the crown. He needs this symbol after the disaster around Uriah and Bathsheba. And I need him to see me as his loyal servant. His letter about Uriah gives me some power over him if I use it well, but he is king and could if he wanted find a way to make me take the blame, letter or not.

We have made an agreement with the Ammonites concerning the amount they will give to Israel. Having them as tributaries will help pay for the various things David has in mind to do in the capital and in the nation, as well as maintain this army that I spend all my time with! It takes a lot of soldiers to keep peace on such extensive borders as ours.

We have destroyed the fortifications of this city and will do the same to the other cities of the Ammonites. I do not want to have to deal with such resistance again.

Your loving son,
Joab

3.14 Amnon and Tamar
Abigail (at Jerusalem) writes to her sister Sarah (at Bethel)

Dear sister,
A terrible thing has happened here, something worse than anyone could have anticipated.

There has been much friction in the family of late that David has seemed unwilling or unable to confront. The children of different mothers are frequently in conflict. Much of this is in anticipation of David's death and his naming of a successor. Amnon, as the firstborn, has been the one expected to succeed David, but this has not been popular with some in the family. Amnon has been considered by many to be a young man with no sense of restraint. His mother will not control him; she has never been a strong person. And since the incident with Uriah, David has not taken a strong hand with his children himself.

Amnon fell in love with Tamar, sister to Absalom. Of course, this is a difficult situation, but there have been cases of a half-brother and half-sister marrying. The rest of the family didn't know Amnon's feelings for Tamar. He is not close to the other sons, who have no respect for him. But he spoke to his friends and worked out a scheme to do an awful thing.

He pretended to be ill, and David visited him to see what could be done. Amnon asked that Tamar come to his house to cook for him. David agreed to this and she went. When she had prepared the food, Amnon sent everyone else away and asked her to bring it to him in his bed. He then grabbed her and raped her.

After he had her, his feelings changed, and he threw her out of his house. Surely he was ashamed of what he had done and in his mind made her the guilty one. Tamar tore her garments and put ashes on her head, so everyone knew she was in deep distress about something.

Her brother Absalom suspected the cause and that it had been done by Amnon. When he asked, Tamar said it was true. She wept and said she tried to tell Amnon he should speak to David, who would not stand in the way of their marrying, but Amnon would not listen or wait. Absalom took her to his house where she remains a woman without hope. No man will want anything to do with her after this.

David is incensed but does nothing. He loves Amnon and makes too many concessions because Amnon is his heir. I have never confronted David before, but we have had several violent arguments about this matter. It is outrageous that he will not act. I want him to deal with Amnon, who deserves severe punishment. He should be disinherited.

David believes that God has forgiven him for his own sins in the matter of Uriah and Bathsheba. But even so he seems to lack the conviction to express moral judgment on his children or others in the kingdom. This leaves the family and the nation in a weak and dangerous position. If David will not lead and stand up to evil because he believes he lacks the moral authority to do so, anything can happen. Well, Amnon has demonstrated how bad it can be.

It's well known in the family that even though Absalom has advised Tamar to suffer in silence, and even though he does not speak to Amnon at all, he hates Amnon for what was done. The act was despicable, and Absalom's strong feelings make this a dangerous situation. I know that we are not done with the matter yet.

As I get older and the family becomes larger and the problems more complicated, I find myself wanting to withdraw. I long for the simplicity – even with the hardships – of the days when I met David in the desert of Judah and became his wife. I hardly recognize that David in the man who now heads this family and rules this nation. I will continue to fight him on this until he acts, as the David of the desert would have done.

With love,
Abigail

3.15 Tamar's Suffering
Tamar (at Jerusalem) writes to her aunt, Zeruiah (at Bethlehem)

Aunt,

I'm coming to see you tomorrow. I need to leave the palace and the city. There is no peace for me here and perhaps never will be again. Joab has told me that you can help.

You know what Amnon did to me. I am suffering physically and emotionally. I can't tell you what this is like, this feeling of worthlessness and the horror of thinking – about anything, especially about my future. I want to be avenged. I want Amnon to be hurt, as I have been hurt. I hate him for what he has done to me! I can't think beyond that. Yet I'm powerless to make anything happen.

My mother is worthless to me in this. She has never been a force in the family, accepted only because of the alliance that she brought my father when he was young and in need of supporters. Her father would act, I think, even against the king and his son, but he's in his home city and too old to come. My mother never dealt with my brother Absalom when he needed it, and she's never been able to do anything with my father except sleep with him. I can expect no more than sympathy from her. I hate her for her weakness and her acquiescence, only doing what my father expects her to do!

The women of the family have tried to comfort me, but they are powerless to deal with the situation. I hate this powerlessness, and I hate them for accepting it. Abigail at least tried to talk to David, but he would not even answer her.

Absalom cares more for his own ambitions than for me. He expects being the king's son to have consequences for him. He doesn't realize that being the king's daughter is quite a different matter. And now I'm afraid he sees me only as a way to advance his own ends. I have no idea how he will try to turn this to his advantage, but he surely will as he does with everything. I hate him for his manipulations and his selfish indifference to my pain.

My father is doing nothing! He sits in a daze, more concerned about himself than me. Or more concerned about something – I don't know what he's thinking because he's not talking to me. He seems not to realize what this is like for me; he has shown me no compassion. I've begged and I've wept, and now he will not even see me. I hate him for his lack of love, or at least any expression of it, and for his lack of action. He has done nothing to punish Amnon, which I cannot understand or accept. Amnon deserves to be punished, and my father has not even chastized him. Where is the king who rules this country? He will not even rule his own family. Is this what his God wants from him? I can't believe that.

I can't think without reliving the awfulness of the experience. Amnon was violent and hurt me – but even worse was to be cast away after. Who will have anything to do with a woman whose own family will not defend her? I can only expect to be avoided and spurned, or at best pitied. I can't bear to think about what my life will be like, and how different from what I have grown up to expect. What will I become? What will the story of Tamar be? Will I be remembered by future generations of this family only as the woman raped and discarded by her brother – or can I possibly be more?

This is what I want to talk to you about. I need help, and I know you are a strong woman. Although we have not been close, I hope that you will receive me and let me stay with you until I can overcome the anger and the fear and the hatred that now fills me.

In desperation,
Tamar

3.16 Absalom Kills Amnon

Ahinoam (at Jerusalem) writes to her sister Milcah (at Jezreel)

Sister –
Come to me at once – I need you desperately.

My son Amnon is dead – at the hand of his own brother!

These past two years have been terrible, knowing what my son did to Tamar and being ashamed of him and of my husband for not dealing with him. But though David ignored it, Absalom did not. He has nurtured his hatred for Amnon and now has killed him!

How the thing was done is typical of Absalom and his subtlety. He invited David and all the other sons to a celebration at the annual shearing of his sheep. David refused the invitation but allowed his sons to go, including Amnon, who was specifically invited by Absalom. This might have been some hint that something was not usual! Who knows – perhaps David did sense that something would happen and for that reason stayed away.

When everyone had feasted and drunk too much, Absalom had his servants kill Amnon. He did not even do the deed himself!

The first news of it made us think that all our sons were dead, but of course it was only my poor, foolish Amnon. David mourns now for his first-born and his hope for establishing a dynasty. But he mourns alone, and so do I. I cannot take comfort from a man who would not deal with one foolish son – a rapist – and now will not deal with another son – a murderer! Absalom has taken refuge in his maternal grandfather's house, and David seems content to leave him there and ignore him.

How has David come to this? How has our family come to this? I have lost my son, and my husband and I have no comfort for each other! I've been weeping alone through the days and feeling even more alone through the nights.

Come, please.

In despair,
Ahinoam

3.17 Absalom Returns from Exile
Joab (at Rabbah) writes to his mother, Zeruiah (at Bethlehem)

Dear Mother,

I've acted on your advice about forcing the king to deal with the issue of Absalom. His mourning over Amnon was replaced by mourning over Absalom's banishment, so that he was hardly able to govern the nation.

I did as you said and hired a wise woman to meet with David. I was present in court when she appeared. She told him a story supposedly about her own family. She said that one of her two sons had killed the other and now her only remaining son was subject to the death penalty. Her family would be destroyed if this happened. David promised to intervene on her behalf to protect the remaining son.

Once he committed himself to this, she revealed that her story was intended to make him realize what he was doing himself. Her reputation for wisdom is well deserved! She told him that his action was not good for the people of God and further implied that

God is more gracious to sinners than David has been himself. She did not mention Absalom by name, but the message was clear.

I had told her what end I wanted to achieve but left it to her to decide how to bring it about. Her appeal to David's faith was brilliant. Of course he sees himself as acting for the welfare of Israel, so any hint that his action is not good for the people commands his attention. And her argument about the graciousness of God was particularly strong. The king knows that his own action with Uriah merited the death penalty, a penalty that was not applied either by God or by the nation. He has been unable to deal with Absalom because he could not decide between justice – Absalom's death – and mercy – forgiving him and letting him return home. So I was very impressed with this woman; she was worth all I paid.

David is no fool, though, even in the indecisive state of these recent years. He asked the woman if I was the one who had sent her to him. When she admitted that I was, he turned to me. I feared he would be angry, but he simply told me to bring Absalom back to Jerusalem. He will be confined to his own house and the king will not see him. But it's a start, and I'm away immediately to fetch him home.

Your loving son,
Joab

3.18 David Meets with Absalom
Joab (at Rabbah) writes to his mother, Zeruiah (at Bethlehem)

Dear Mother,
We've manipulated the king to bring Absalom back to Israel, and now Absalom has manipulated me!

Two years ago we tried to rouse David from his lethargy by forcing him to bring Absalom back from exile. But Absalom has lived in isolation from the court since then. His family has grown, and he has been a strong presence in the community, but still the king would not see him.

Absalom sent word that he wanted to talk to me. Knowing the king's views, I refused. So he sent his servants to set fire to my crops, and of course I *had* to speak with him then. He wanted me to intercede with the King on his behalf. He is angry at being in Jerusalem but living in limbo. Brash as ever, he claimed that if there is guilt, the king should kill him! He knows that David's decision two years ago was motivated partly by his own sense of having been forgiven when guilty. I saw his desire to have his position restored, but I could not tell if he has any love for David.

Nonetheless, I agreed to speak to David on Absalom's behalf. David summoned him to what was a dramatic meeting, as you might expect. Absalom prostrated himself before the king, and David raised and kissed him. So Absalom has now been welcomed back into the court and its activities.

Yet neither of them has referred to the cause of all of this trouble. And what's not been mentioned festers between them. David knows he should forgive Absalom but has not been able to say it, perhaps because Absalom has not asked for forgiveness. Absalom resents that David has never condemned Amnon's act even to Absalom or Tamar. David's subsequent lack of action towards Absalom is also a source of resentment with Absalom himself. I do not see a solid basis for a restored family and court life in this.

I want to talk at length to you about these matters. I'll arrange to be away for a few days towards the end of the month and will come home then. If Abishai can be free, I'll being him with me.

Your loving son,
Joab

3.19 Absalom Conspires against David
Joab (at Jerusalem) writes to his mother, Zeruiah (at Bethlehem)

Dear Mother,
I write in haste, as so often. We've just received word that Absalom is setting himself up as king in Hebron, where he went on pretence of paying a vow to the Lord for his return to the city after that business over Amnon. It's ironic he's chosen that place, reminiscent of David's rule over Judah before the kingdom was reunited. I hope he's not trying to renew the tension between Judah and Israel that David has worked so well to remove.

But this should have been anticipated. Since his reconciliation with David and the end of his house arrest, he's been looking for power and recognition. In my opinion he's been looking for trouble too. He's had a habit of sitting at the gate of Jerusalem to be the first one seen by people coming to court for help. He's famous for his glorious long hair, of course, and that would certainly catch people's attention. He'd listen to their problems, and commiserate that the king and the court would be too busy to deal with them. If he were king, of course, things would be different. He treated them like his friends, and they responded well to him. It looked dangerous to me, but David ignored it.

What's happened now can't be ignored. We hear that Absalom has already sent messengers to several of David's officials looking for their support. David has not yet drawn his advisors together, so I don't know how he'll react. I hope, though, to be gone from here by evening with the army to Hebron to deal with this upstart.

Your loving son,
Joab

3.20 David Flees from Absalom
Abiathar the priest (at Jerusalem) writes to Gad the prophet (at Ramah)

Fellow-servant,
I know that you have longed for this period of retreat with the other prophets, but you must set that thought aside and return to Jerusalem immediately. The king has had word of a rebellion by Absalom, centred in Hebron where he said he was going to make a sacrifice. Now the king has fled into the desert!

I know this will amaze you. Shortly after the news from Hebron, another messenger came, this one saying there was a great deal of popular support for Absalom. I don't know where that man came from. Perhaps David had sent the fellow himself to see what was stirring. And perhaps it was his sense of the people turning away from him that made him leave. Joab was ready for a battle, but David would not let it happen here and now.

Most of the court and even some visitors have gone with him. I went with him along with some other priests out of the city, carrying the Ark. But David sent us back before climbing into the mountains to the east towards the desert. He was weeping as he went.

Just before we left him, he received news that Absalom has convinced Ahithophel to switch his allegiance and become his advisor. That is a loss to David, because he has trusted Ahithophel in many matters.

Hushai was also part of the entourage leaving with David. But when David heard the news about Ahithophel, he asked Hushai to return to Jerusalem to wait for Absalom's arrival. He told Hushai to give advice contrary to Ahithophel's. This will be a difficult thing for him to do, as these two have been together in advising the king for so long. Hushai is also to send news of developments to David through those of us in the temple who remain loyal to David as the Lord's anointed king. Our sons will act as messengers to reach David in the desert.

He made these plans quickly, without stopping to work out details. There was no time for a meeting of the council or discussion. Perhaps he wants to make himself the one being chased rather than chasing Absalom, and thus win back some sympathy among the people. Absalom may be trying to revive memories of David's youth when he was the hero in Hebron, wanted by the people. David may be attempting to thwart that.

He may be at least in part motivated by a longing for those days when he was in the wilderness and in control of his life. Then he was unfettered with the affairs of the kingdom, living with his family and his thousand. There has surely been little pleasure for him in Jerusalem in recent years.

Or he may also want to avoid fighting against his own son and be hoping for some reconciliation. He seems always to have expected great things of Absalom, though there's been no evidence of anything but scheming from that one!

Whatever is in David's mind, he has kept it to himself. He's gone, and you and I are among the few faithful that have been left behind. I need you with me. When this reaches you, it will be too late to start out, but please leave at first light in the morning.

Under the mercy,
Abiathar

3.21 David's Meditation: Fleeing from Absalom
David writes in the desert

O Lord, how many are my foes!
   Many are rising against me;
many are saying to me,
   "There is no help for you in God."

But you, O Lord, are a shield around me,
   my glory, and the one who lifts up my head.
I cry aloud to the Lord,
   and he answers me from his holy hill.

I lie down and sleep;
   I wake again, for the Lord sustains me.
I am not afraid of ten thousands of people
   who have set themselves against me all around.

Rise up, O Lord!
   Deliver me, O my God!
For you strike all my enemies on the cheek;
   you break the teeth of the wicked.

Deliverance belongs to the Lord;
   may your blessing be on your people!

3.22 Ziba Assists David
Abigail (at Jerusalem) writes to her sister Sarah (at Bethel)

Dear sister,
Another disaster, and we're on the move again. I'm scribbling this as we take a brief rest on the summit of the Mount of Olives to muster a group that's been hurriedly put together. Absalom is leading a rebellion against David, and rather than fight him, we're heading into the desert to the east – most of the court and all of the family. I don't know what's ahead so I can't tell you where we'll be or when you'll hear from me. The news arrived and immediately David decided to move. I don't know what he intends, but at least he's taking charge.

It's not clear who stands where. There are some surprises. Ziba, the servant of Mephibosheth, has just been here to hand over supplies to David: bread, fruit, and wine. But apparently Mephibosheth has decided that this might be an opportunity to have the throne returned to the house of Saul and in particular to him, so he's waiting in Jerusalem for Absalom's arrival.

Pray for us, back in the wilderness after so many years.

With love,
Abigail

3.23 Shimei Curses David
Abishai (at Jerusalem) writes to his mother, Zeruiah (at Bethlehem)

Dear Mother,
I know that Joab wrote to you today, but I send this as well since I've no way of knowing when I'll see you again. We've stopped briefly on the summit of the Mount of Olives to gather the company, which has become quite scattered in the rush to get out of the city and up here on our way to the desert.

This is a strange and sudden change in our lives, and especially for David. For years he's been used to praises from the people and the deference given to a king, but things are different today. A kinsman of Saul named Shimei came out to curse him, saying this rebellion results from David's being a man of blood. He doubtless still believes those rumours about David being responsible for the deaths of Saul and Jonathan, and possibly also Abner.

I wanted to cut down the worthless fool, but David wouldn't let me. The Lord had sent Shimei to curse him, he said, and God would repay good for the evil of this cursing. I think he meant that God would look on him with favour because he was being cursed without justification. It's as if he wanted something that was *unjust* to happen to him to attract God's attention to him for good, because being driven out of Jerusalem was a justifiable punishment for other things he'd done. Perhaps he had in mind his failure to deal with his sons, or his murder of Uriah. I don't know. And it looks like this fool Shimei intends to follow us as we continue on our way, at least for some part of the distance.

Enough. Mother, David is a great campaigner when he wants to fight. And Joab is the best general in the land, so we're at an advantage no matter whom Absalom attracts to his cause. I am confident we'll be back but I don't know when. If possible we'll get messengers to you from time to time, and will look for your letters in return.

With love,
Abishai

3.24 Absalom Receives Conflicting Advice
Abiathar the priest (at Jerusalem) writes to Gad the prophet (at Ramah)

Fellow-servant,
I was extremely disappointed that you were too ill to return with my messenger, and I pray you are recovering. I still want you back here as soon as possible, as do others. These are confusing times: we must maintain a show of support for Absalom while working for the Lord's truly anointed king. But until you return I will send messengers so that you can be informed and be thinking about what should be done. Any advice you have can be sent back with the messengers.

Absalom's arrival in the city drew crowds, as you can imagine. Ahithophel was already with Absalom, and Hushai came out to meet them and to offer his services as advisor. Absalom was suspicious, I think, but accepted Hushai's assurance that he would serve the king the people supported.

Absalom's pride caused him not to probe any further with Hushai. I was nearby when this interchange occurred and I knew that Hushai was worried, but he handled it well. Ahithophel has always been matchless as an advisor to David. Hushai needs to thwart Absalom and Ahithophel by giving advice that will be acceptable to Absalom but will allow David opportunities to save himself and eventually to defeat Absalom.

Ahithophel suggested immediately to Absalom that he should set up a tent in full view of the people and should take there David's concubines who had been left behind. This Absalom did. Once it had been established in such a clear way that Absalom was in charge in the king's household, they turned to planning how to deal with David.

I was with them again for that discussion, and Ahithophel was brilliant. He urged that a small force be assembled immediately to pursue David in the wilderness. Because of the king's age and weariness, the force would quickly overtake him and easily subdue him. Since the focus was only on one man, David, the matter could be settled quickly. There need not be much bloodshed, and thus Absalom would retain the support of the people.

The wisdom of this was easy to see. It was not clear to me how Hushai could turn this plan aside, and it was all too clear that if Ahithophel's plan were put into action, David would be taken by morning and probably killed.

But the Lord was with us, and Hushai was amazing to watch and hear. He said that Ahithophel's advice was bad. He described David as a great warrior accompanied by great warriors, in circumstances with which he is very familiar. He would not easily be found because he would have separated himself from the company and gone into hiding. There would inevitably be a fight, and some of Absalom's men would be killed. Then the people of Israel would remember David's exploits years ago in the desert. The stories of that time are almost legends now! And remembering those old stories, the people would begin to think that Absalom could not hold the kingdom against David.

So, Hushai said, Absalom should instead take the time to gather a large army from the entire nation. This army would be sufficient to follow David anywhere, lay siege to any city where he might take refuge, and deal with any obstacle encountered on the campaign to capture and subdue David. This too sounded like good advice, though in fact it would give David time to escape further into the desert.

Absalom and his close supporters preferred Hushai's advice. I suspect they are afraid of David, and the description of this great warrior in the wilderness at night evidently magnified their fears! But behind that human reaction, I know the Lord was at work to thwart Ahithophel's good advice.

We sent messengers to David. They had some difficulty because they were seen, but they successfully eluded their pursuers and got the word to David. They have returned with news that he has now hurried east to the Jordan and across it. There he hopes to find allies and supplies for all those with him.

An amazing development has just occurred. Ahithophel was so distressed at having his advice rejected by Absalom that he went home and hanged himself.

Absalom had gained credibility by having Ahithophel with him. Now Absalom has been undermined in two ways. First, by spurning Ahithophel he has lost an excellent advisor. Second, it will now be apparent to the people that Absalom alienated someone with a reputation for wisdom. And now Hushai will be Absalom's chief advisor. It will require some subtlety for him to give advice that Absalom sees to be wise but at the same time leaves room for advantage to David.

One other thing I must tell you. This is important, too. Absalom knows that Joab is not popular with the people and often not with his own troops. He is a ruthless and ambitious man who does not mind pushing his men or shedding blood. David has himself complained of how difficult Joab can be. Absalom has appointed Amasa, who is also, like Joab, a nephew of David, as leader of his army. This will be very popular with the army and with the people. Amasa is not as experienced in command as Joab, but he will make a good leader. Further, his appointment shows there is strong support for Absalom from David's own family and his own tribe of Judah. This is a complication. Absalom's rebellion is not just a family feud between father and son. David will have to deal with this larger reality at some point, assuming he can stay safe and be victorious.

If you have advice for me, I would very much like to have it. As I said, and you can tell for yourself, this is a difficult and dangerous situation. I am trying to encourage Hushai in his work with Absalom. I look forward to your return.

Under the mercy,
Abiathar

3.25 Joab Kills Absalom

Joab (at Mahanaim) writes to his mother, Zeruiah (at Bethlehem)

Dear Mother,
This is a day of victory, a day of glory! We have put down the rebellion of Absalom by defeating his forces. I myself killed the fool, thus ending the battle. Abishai also gained glory for his part in it. It happened like this.

We have been at Mahanaim where David has allies so we were able to provision and prepare to meet Absalom's force. The king himself wanted to go to the battle, but we would not let him. If anything happened to him, there would be no focus and Absalom would have won the throne. David agreed to stay behind, but he did not like it.

As we left he commanded those of us in charge to protect Absalom from harm. It was a foolish thing to say, prompted by his affection for the boy, an affection that has caused him great personal pain and that allowed this rebellion to develop. He had clearly not thought of the consequences. It was obvious to me that Absalom must die.

During the battle Absalom was separated from his troops and discovered by some of ours. He had been trying to ride away but became caught in the forest. That hair of which he was so proud led to his destruction! It got tangled in branches, and his mule went on and left him hanging there.

All the men had heard David's orders as we left, so none had touched him. When I learned he was caught in the tree I myself took three spears and thrust them into his heart. I then had my guard take him down and make sure he was dead. We threw him in a pit and buried him under a pile of stones.

I'm sending you this note before heading back to Mahanaim to meet David. We're a long way from there. I've sent messengers to him so he'll know by now. I'm sure I can expect some harsh words when I get back. He'll not take it well that I disobeyed him. But, as on other occasions, this won't last. Once he's recovered from the shock, he'll see that to protect his position as king, Absalom had to die.

I expect we'll be back in Jerusalem as soon as the company can prepare for the journey. Some will go tomorrow, but I will stay with David and provide his personal protection. My position in court will be even more powerful as a result of this day's work.

If you have advice for me now, send it back with my messenger. Abishai asks me to send his love to you as well.

Your loving son,
Joab

3.26 David's Meditation: Lament for Absalom
David weeps in the desert

O my son Absalom, my son, my son Absalom!
Would I had died instead of you, O Absalom, my son, my son!

3.27 David in Mourning
Ahinoam (at Mahanaim) writes to her sister Milcah (at Jezreel)

Dear sister,
No word from you since we left Jerusalem so quickly and you returned home. I hope you were clear of the city before Absalom's force arrived. I'm sure I would have heard if you'd been captured, so I assume you must be safe. We are no longer under battle conditions here so I write to let you know I am well, and will write further when we return to Jerusalem.

The conflict ended today when Joab killed Absalom in battle. Those of us who had remained in the city spent the time watching for messengers or for the troops to return. Absalom was said to have the larger force but certainly less experience. Eventually we saw two runners coming, separated by a long distance. The first reported victory, which was a relief to all of us, and probably to our hosts here as well, who would like to be clear of all this internal conflict of Israel's.

But there was no news of Absalom from the first runner. Instead of being calmed by the news, David became more agitated. The second runner arrived to confirm the news of the victory but also to say that Absalom was dead. We were all shocked, because we knew of David's explicit command to the generals to spare Absalom. When David heard this news, he left us and went to his room. He could be heard weeping and crying out that he wished he had died instead of Absalom. It was an awful sound. The people were moved by it, and no one was willing to approach him. Even the soldiers as they returned became aware of it and went quietly to their billets.

But when Joab came back, he went directly to see David. Apparently he told him that the soldiers and the people needed to see that the king appreciated the victory that had been won and the valour of the soldiers. He accused David of being more concerned about Absalom than about his entire army. At that David emerged, the troops were assembled, and he reviewed them.

I was afraid of Absalom, afraid of what he might do to the country if he became king and what he might do to me as the mother of Amnon if he captured me. His hatred of his brother had not died. In spite of how he presented himself to the people during recent years, he has been a continuing source of problems and strife within the family and the court. So the victory has meant a great relief for me. I am also shocked to see David so broken by this. There are many emotions involved in his response, I expect. I've never before seen him so distraught in any circumstance that he couldn't see what was needed from him as king. At the same time I am angry with him, and bitter. He was not moved like this when Amnon died. This display is over the man who killed my son!

What is wrong with David? Amnon deserved punishment for what he did to Tamar, and David did not act. Then Absalom murdered Amnon, and David did not act. Now the grief he shows is for the murderer, not for the son who was murdered. Has he lost all sense of what is necessary to discipline a family? Or a nation? I dare not speak to him or be in his presence because I am so angry.

So we survive, but it will take time to recover. And what will be recovered will be some new configuration of emotion and power within the family and the court. This has been a horrible experience for us all. I do not know how it will change David. I hope that his pain will make him more aware of my pain over Amnon.

With love,
Ahinoam

3.28 David's Return to Jerusalem
Abigail (at Jerusalem) writes to her sister Sarah (at Bethel)

Dear sister,
We have returned to our own city and our own home almost like conquerors. Now this place that was so familiar seems somehow different. I care more for the pleasure of simply being here than about the city's importance as the capital.

David is reawakened. He knows how close he came to losing his kingdom, and that has caught his attention as nothing has for some time. He is concerned over his own position and that of the family, of course. But he also carries, I think, a large burden in the sense of the responsibility he feels as the Lord's anointed king. For him there is little difference between his faith and his kingship. He sees the Lord as the ultimate ruler of Israel and himself, or any other king, as regent.

The old conflicts among the twelve tribes of Israel were too much in evidence today. We heard that the people wanted David back as king after he defeated Absalom. But there had been no contact with the leaders of the people. David sent a message to the elders of our own tribe of Judah asking why they were not doing anything about bringing him back.

He also sent a message to Amasa, whom Absalom had made commander of his forces, confirming that henceforth he would be David's commander. This will not sit well with Joab. But Joab so clearly defied David's orders concerning Absalom that severe discipline is required. And it will be a popular decision. Joab is known as a great warrior but not as a man to be trusted. His reputation is that he will maintain his own and David's power at any cost.

In response to David's two messages, Amasa came with the elders of Judah – but no other leaders – to escort David back to Jerusalem. I suspect David had wanted Judah not to act alone but to spur on all the leaders to bring him back. And as we crossed the Jordan River, many from the other tribes joined the procession, cheering at David's return.

But when we got to Gilgal, there was trouble. Some from the remaining tribes were angry with the Judahites for acting without them. A vigorous argument broke out, but I thought it would die down with all the people coming together to support David. Then that worthless Sheba of Saul's tribe of Benjamin started to speak. Perhaps he was still nursing old resentments about David's defeat of the house of Saul. He called out that the tribes of Israel should have nothing to do with David. All the dissenters left with this wretch. I do not think we've heard the last of this.

Then Shimei, who had cursed David so vigorously as we left the city, showed up to apologize and ask for forgiveness. David promised him that he would live. In the company with him were a number of others from the tribe of Benjamin, hoping to restore themselves in David's sight and presumably wanting to reduce any suspicion that they still harbour hopes for a king from Saul's family.

Among them was Ziba, Mephibosheth's servant, along with all his family. He had given David supplies when we left Jerusalem, saying that his master was not coming out because he hoped to become king himself. These people were particularly ingratiating. And Mephibosheth himself was there, looking awful. He had not washed or changed his clothes since David left Jerusalem. Ziba had tricked him on the day we left, Mephibosheth claimed, and had gone off with a false description of what his master was doing.

I think David was growing tired of this. The conflict with the tribe of Benjamin and Saul's family has been drawn out and fruitless for both sides. Rather than decide between the two of them, he gave each half the estate that Mephibosheth had previously held.

We also had Barzillai with us for part of the trip. He's an old man now, like many of David's supporters. He supplied us with much of what we needed during the time we were away from the city. David wanted to bring him back to Jerusalem, but he preferred to return to his own place and people.

David will have to deal with Sheba, and there will be care required to rebuild a base of support for keeping the nation unified under his leadership. I had wished for something to move David out of his lethargy and bring the family together, but I certainly did not want civil war to be the stimulus. I hope my last years can be peaceful, that this will be the last campaign in which we participate directly. David may long for the years in the desert, but I like the comforts of the city.

With love,
Abigail

3.29 Sheba Rebels

Abishai (at Jerusalem) writes to his mother, Zeruiah (at Bethlehem)

Dear Mother,

My brother is either a fool or a madman.

After our return to Jerusalem, David confirmed Amasa as head of the army, and Joab, of course, was furious! He had hoped that his killing of Absalom would make David value him more highly. He had thought that David's promise to Amasa was simply a negotiating stance that would be set aside as soon as we returned. He hasn't learned after all these years anything at all of what David is like. When David has given a promise, it stands.

David also asked Amasa to gather the army together in three days to pursue Sheba. Joab was eager to get to the fight, and when Amasa did not return in three days, Joab decided that he and I would lead those available in search of Sheba. We had not gone far when Amasa and his troops met us. As we stopped to make plans, Joab walked up to Amasa. But rather than talking, he grabbed Amasa by the beard and stabbed him to death. The men were shocked. I myself could not have imagined Joab would do this.

To distract the men, we immediately left in pursuit of Sheba. We found where he had hidden and besieged the place. Joab set about battering down the wall. But a wise woman called from the wall to ask him what he was doing. When he explained about Sheba, she disappeared, and in a short time Sheba's head was thrown out over the wall. Joab called off the siege and sent the soldiers home.

We returned to Jerusalem where David was in the middle of setting up his new court. Of course, he expected to have Amasa as commander of the army. In part this would have been to fulfil his promise but in part to bind those who supported Absalom more closely to the new regime. He was pleased to hear that Sheba had been killed and the rebellion put down, but he was furious with Joab for having killed Amasa. He had not had news of that before because Joab would not let any messengers return until he was ready to come back with the news of the victory himself.

I don't understand my brother. Surely by now he should have learned something about David! He has been confirmed, as he desired, as commander of the army once again, but he is out of favour with David. If there was another choice, I believe that David would have made it. I'm disappointed to realize that he does not have confidence in me to do the job.

I have never wanted the larger role that Joab has played, but I've often felt that I had the ability to do it. Joab's defiance of David's order will undermine his authority with the troops, so a change should be made. I'm overlooked, I believe, because David wants neither of us "sons of Zeruiah," as he calls us, and it is easier to stick with the one in place than to change to the other.

With love,
Abishai

3.30 Vengeance on Saul's House
Michal (at Jerusalem) writes to her cousin Marah (at Gibeah)

My cousin,
I begin to wonder if the conflict between the houses of Saul and David will ever end. David has delivered seven of our kinsmen to their deaths.

The famine of these past three years has been so severe that David prayed to the Lord to tell him what to do. It was revealed to him that there was blood guilt on the house of Saul because of my father's attempt to eliminate the Gibeonites from their enclave in the middle of Israel. At least, David said that this was revealed to him! So he went to the Gibeonites to settle the issue. They did not want money, they said, but instead demanded that seven men of the house of Saul be given to them to be put to death.

Had David anticipated this? It would be surprising to me if he had not gained some information about their expectations before meeting with them. But whether he knew in advance or not, he was now in a position of having asked what was required and almost being forced to give it. If he didn't convey these ideas of his as if they came from the Lord, he would be able to back away from them when things don't go as he would like.

So in the circumstances David agreed to this awful request! He gave them seven men – excluding Mephibosheth, of course, because of his promise. But he sent the two sons that the concubine Rizpah bore to my father and the five sons of my sister Merab, who was offered to him as his wife when he defeated Goliath! The Gibeonites executed them cruelly by impaling them on stakes at the top of a mountain, and left the bodies there.

Rizpah is such a strong woman! She went and sat by the bodies night and day, not allowing the birds or animals to feed on them. David heard of this and, embarrassed by it, sent to retrieve the bodies. He also collected the remains of Saul and Jonathan from the Israelites who had stolen them back from the Philistines. He had all these bodies buried in the land that belongs to our tribe of Benjamin. So at last my father and my brother have come home.

Will it be over now? Will David and those around him feel secure enough to stop persecuting our family? How large a price must be paid by the vanquished? What happened to the guileless young man I loved? I'm ill from the brutality of it all. You can imagine how this affects the relationships I have with others in the family and the court, relationships that are not smooth at best.

In love and sorrow,
Michal

3.31 More Philistine Battles
Abishai (at Jerusalem) writes to his mother, Zeruiah (at Bethlehem)

Dear Mother,
More victories for Israel! And in these latest, I have had my own part. Since Absalom's rebellion, our enemies have been testing David's strength. Our latest forays have been against the Philistines. David was on the battlefield himself and was almost killed, but I protected him and slew his attacker. The camp is talking about it still. I believe David himself is thankful, but he has difficulty expressing this to me because of his continuing anger at my brother.

Afterwards, all the generals agreed that the king must in future be kept away from the battles, and told him so. He is too valuable to lose. The kingdom would be in chaos, and our enemies would run over us. He is also too old and slow to be in the fighting himself.

In the last few days we've killed more of the best warriors among the Philistines. I think they'll go back home and leave us now. They needed to see if they could return to their pattern of raids against our western lands, but we've shown them it's not safe.

Like David, I myself am beginning to feel too old to fight. So many battles, and what have we accomplished? Joab lives for the conflict, but I wish only to see a better life secured for my children.

With love,
Abishai

3.32 David's Meditation: Praise for Victory
David writes at Jerusalem

> The Lord is my rock, my fortress, and my deliverer,
>   my God, my rock, in whom I take refuge,
> my shield and the horn of my salvation,
>   my stronghold and my refuge,
>   my saviour; you save me from violence.
> I call upon the Lord, who is worthy to be praised,
>   and I am saved from my enemies.

For the waves of death encompassed me,
> the torrents of perdition assailed me;
the cords of Sheol entangled me,
> the snares of death confronted me.

In my distress I called upon the Lord;
> to my God I called.
From his temple he heard my voice,
> and my cry came to his ears.

Then the earth reeled and rocked;
> the foundations of the heavens trembled
> and quaked, because he was angry.
Smoke went up from his nostrils,
> And devouring fire from his mouth;
> glowing coals flamed forth from him.
He bowed the heavens, and came down;
> thick darkness was under his feet.
He rode on a cherub, and flew;
> he was seen upon the wings of the wind.
He made darkness around him a canopy,
> thick clouds, a gathering of water.
Out of the brightness before him
> coals of fire flamed forth.
The Lord thundered from heaven;
> the Most High uttered his voice.
He sent out arrows, and scattered them
> – lightning, and routed them.
Then the channels of the sea were seen,
> the foundations of the world were laid bare
at the rebuke of the Lord,
> at the blast of the breath of his nostrils.

He reached from on high, he took me,
> he drew me out of mighty waters.
He delivered me from my strong enemy,
> from those who hated me;
> for they were too mighty for me.
They came upon me in the day of my calamity,
> but the Lord was my stay.

He brought me out into a broad place;
    he delivered me, because he delighted in me.

The Lord rewarded me according to my righteousness;
    according to the cleanness of my hands he recompensed me.
For I have kept the ways of the Lord,
    and have not wickedly departed from my God.
For all his ordinances were before me,
    and from his statutes I did not turn aside.
I was blameless before him,
    and I kept myself from guilt.
Therefore the Lord has recompensed me according to my righteousness,
    according to my cleanness in his sight.

With the loyal you show yourself loyal;
    with the blameless you show yourself blameless;
with the pure you show yourself pure,
    and with the crooked you show yourself perverse.
You deliver a humble people,
    but your eyes are upon the haughty to bring them down.
Indeed, you are my lamp, O Lord,
    the Lord lightens my darkness.
By you I can crush a troop,
    and by my God I can leap over a wall.
This God – his way is perfect;
    the promise of the Lord proves true;
    he is a shield for all who take refuge in him.

For who is God, but the Lord?
    And who is a rock, except our God?
The God who has girded me with strength
    has opened wide my path.
He made my feet like the feet of deer,
    and set me secure on the heights.
He trains my hands for war,
    so that my arms can bend a bow of bronze.

You have given me the shield of your salvation,
    and your help has made me great.

You have made me stride freely,
   and my feet do not slip;
I pursued my enemies and destroyed them,
   and did not turn back until they were consumed.
I consumed them; I struck them down, so that they did not rise;
   they fell under my feet.
For you girded me with strength for the battle;
   you made my assailants sink under me.
You made my enemies turn their backs to me,
   those who hated me, and I destroyed them.
They looked, but there was no one to save them;
   they cried to the Lord, but he did not answer them.
I beat them fine like the dust of the earth,
    I crushed them and stamped them down like the mire of
      the streets.

You delivered me from strife with the peoples;
   you kept me as the head of the nations;
   people whom I had not known served me.
Foreigners came cringing to me;
   as soon as they heard of me, they obeyed me.
Foreigners lost heart,
   and came trembling out of their strongholds.

The Lord lives! Blessed be my rock,
   and exalted be my God, the rock of my salvation,
the God who gave me vengeance
   and brought down peoples under me,
who brought me out from my enemies;
   you exalted me above my adversaries,
   you delivered me from the violent.

For this I will extol you, O Lord, among the nations,
   and sing praises to your name.
He is a tower of salvation for his king,
   and shows steadfast love to his anointed,
   to David and his descendants forever.

4 Dynasty

Zadok the Scribe's Commentary

The previous group of documents covered a period of strong forces and strong passions around David, his court, and his family. The one letter from the hand of Zeruiah makes me understand why David used the term "sons of Zeruiah" to describe those – her sons and others – who were continually involved in intrigue and bloodshed. In the midst of her brother's greatest trouble, she actually contemplated the possible end of his reign, presumably to the advantage of herself and her sons.

In this section I have included some of David's songs to show his own expressions of strong feelings. His confession after the Bathsheba incident is full of sorrow. The startling aspect of that song for me is David's statement to God that "against you, you alone, have I sinned." With all that he had done to Bathsheba, to Uriah, and to the people who trusted him as their leader, how could he see his sin as being only against God? The only way I make sense of this statement is to see David saying to God that in stepping outside the moral guidelines that God has given, he had sinned by assuming that his own choices were better than God's. In this way, he had sinned first and foremost – but only? – against God. I wonder if David sought forgiveness from any of the people he injured?

His lack of expression of any emotion when Tamar was raped also bewilders me. I am appalled by this unfolding tragedy that David did nothing to prevent. Relationships with children can be difficult, I know myself. My own daughter and I have had our differences, especially as I gave increasing time to the work of the temple, and now she seldom comes to me. Even so, I cannot imagine the outrage I would feel if someone attacked her. Did David's guilt over Bathsheba and Uriah incapacitate him even though he had sought forgiveness from God? How could he not respond to his daughter? How can I learn anything useful from this man's life?

Only when his son Absalom is killed does David truly express a father's grief. It should break a man's heart to lose his child. David grieved for Absalom as he had not done for Amnon. I know that it would break my heart to lose my daughter. Perhaps, too, David is pouring the grief accumulated from many terrible events in his family into this lament.

During that period David had tremendous trouble and stress. Much of what had characterized his behaviour earlier in his life and brought him such success was missing. Nevertheless, as he approached the end of his life, David had a large vision of what he wanted to accomplish. He knew that he needed to do this through the agency of others, because he would not accomplish it on his own.

He wanted to establish a temple for the worship of the Lord in Jerusalem. According to the stories passed down to us in the sacred texts and rounded out in these documents, he was not allowed to do so by God because he was a man of war. So he amassed materials that would be used by his successor to build the temple, and he established a pattern of worship and commissioned companies of singers and others to participate in the rituals.

He wanted to establish a dynasty, and so needed to name one of his sons as the next king. He also wanted to make clear how much had been accomplished during his own reign. This is apparently why he decided to have a census of the people.

David's reign encompassed forty years: seven over Judah only, and thirty-three over the unified nation of Israel. Leading a nation is a complex task, and there are always conflicting desires and requirements. It is not surprising that in a reign of that length there would be problems, and that there would be some alienated and disaffected because of decisions that the king had taken. As he prepared to pass rule on to his son, he advised Solomon about some of the potential dangers he would face from those around him. For all his songs and words about the Lord, David was a skilled leader who could see how to manage complex situations even at the end of his life.

What is surprising to me is that the man who had done such awful things and had such great failures in his life still thought that he could legitimately turn to these larger goals. He did all of this in the name of God.

4.01 Census of Warriors
Joab (at Jerusalem) writes to his mother, Zeruiah (at Bethlehem)

Dear Mother,
I've long since learned not to second-guess my own decisions, so I won't look back on this year to question any of my part in it. But I could wish that the king's actions had been different.

When David decided almost a year ago that he wanted a census taken of the fighting men of Israel, I argued against it, as you know. I could see no value in it, and I knew the people would resent it. We have always been able to muster an army when needed, without any complicated records. I know that David thinks we rely too much on informal methods, but they have worked. And he has not needed to tax the people because the tributes from foreign countries have been sufficient to keep his government supplied, so no records were needed for that purpose either. I suspect his pride lay behind this undertaking: he wanted a record of the extent of this kingdom that he has assembled. Whatever his reason, he is king and I was sent to count the people.

My men and I have spent almost a year on this thankless task. Everywhere we have gone, we've been greeted with suspicion, as I had known we would be. Grumbling everywhere, men hiding in some places and needing to be rooted out, a growing suspicion of the king and his motives. Questions we could not answer to their satisfaction: Is the king planning to raise an army to invade a foreign land? Is the king going to take our young men away? Is the king now going to make us pay taxes to support him and his family? It was so tiresome, and the worse for having been predictable. Even many of the fighters from my past campaigns avoided us or, worse, taunted us when we visited their towns and villages.

A week ago we completed the census and reported the numbers to David. He was pleased that day. But on the next, he was overcome with guilt, describing the entire exercise as foolishness and as sin, and confessing it to the Lord! My men were outraged that such unpleasant work, commanded by the king, was now of no value to him. But I thought that at last he was coming to his senses and that though the numbering had been done we would set it aside and not use it.

We were not to get clear of this so easily, though. David's new ideas about the census were confirmed the next day when his seer Gad came before him. In the name of the Lord, Gad offered David a choice among three years of famine, three months of war, or three days of pestilence. Any of these would be considered payment to the Lord for the sin of the census. David said he preferred to fall into the hands of the merciful Lord rather than the hands of men. He thus eliminated the second option but did not choose between the first and third. Gad took this as sufficient answer and left.

The next morning the pestilence broke out, and it raged for three days. I know it has been the cause of deaths among your friends and in our family in Bethlehem. It touched all our towns and villages, but the city of Jerusalem was spared.

Gad then told David to erect an altar on top of the mountain where Araunah threshes his wheat. You know the place, I think, Mother, because I pointed it out to you on one of your visits here. That land overlooks the entire city of Jerusalem. I went there with David. Araunah offered to give him the land, but David insisted on buying it, saying that he would not offer to the Lord something that had cost him nothing.

So he has made his sacrifice, and the plague is over. If he had only taken my advice in the first place, we would not have created all the ill-will there now is in the land over the census and then the plague. The people know that what displeased them also displeased the Lord.

But the Lord, if indeed it was the Lord, has shown mercy to David again. He will make much of that, and he will try to convince the people to accept the confession and sacrifice that the Lord has also accepted. You know that he wants to build a temple for the Lord here in Jerusalem. But he cannot build it himself, the Lord says, because he is a man of war. David expects the next king to build it. And he has found the place for it now, he says. This land he bought from Araunah will be the site of the future temple! He turns every event in his life into something that gives meaning to the future for his kingdom, and something in which he sees the Lord. The people are angry with him for the census and the plague, and he will now present them with this idea: the location of the great temple has been discovered as a result of all of this commotion and death. I do not know if even David can make this an acceptable outcome.

I will be busy with reorganizing my officers for a few days, since I lost some of my most important leaders to the plague. When I have that in hand I will come to see you. I know there were deaths in Bethlehem, but you will have to tell me which of your friends are gone, and we will mourn together.

Your loving son,
Joab

4.02 Adonijah Assumes the Throne
Nathan the prophet (at Jerusalem) writes to Gad the prophet (at Ramah)

Dear colleague,
I have worried that the lack of discipline in David's family would bring about even more trouble than we have seen so far. But the king is not an easy man to rebuke unless I can claim that my words come from God. I've warned him that he has not sufficiently held his sons in check. Adonijah, the third-born after Amnon and Absalom, has been one of the most irresponsible, and yet David would not deal with him. Now he is seeing the result.

It's true that David is old and that his last years have not been particularly glorious. The people begin to wonder about the succession. This has long been a subject of speculation and intrigue at court and in the family. Even some of David's most loyal followers are caught up in it, attempting to make things happen rather than waiting for the king – or, more importantly, for God – to act.

It does not surprise me that Joab would be among the discontented. He has always had his own ideas about how the country should be ruled, and who should do what, and when. So when Adonijah drew Joab into his circle of confidants, it was consistent with Joab's past behaviour. He surely saw Adonijah as the next in line, with Amnon and Absalom both gone. And he surely likes the ambition and the energy that he sees there; Adonijah would be Joab's kind of king. But I was disappointed to know that my friend Abiathar was so impatient for a resolution that he too became part of Adonijah's circle. That had been kept from me.

Today all was revealed. Adonijah took his supporters, being very careful to leave me out and Solomon as well, to offer sacrifices and to proclaim himself the king's successor. The arrogance of it was astonishing. I know that Joab was there without his usual guard, and I can only assume that this is because the army does not want to act without a word from the king, even if Joab is willing to do so.

When I heard of this, I spoke to Bathsheba. Even though David has not made a public announcement, it has been clear for some time that he intends to name her son Solomon as his successor. David has never spoken to me directly about this. However, it has been in the background of several of our conversations about the future of the nation and of the worship of the Lord here in Jerusalem.

I am not sure why David made this choice. Solomon is not a warrior like some of his brothers, and he does not have the brashness of Adonijah. He has spent most of his life as a scholar. Perhaps David believes that the period of war to put down our enemies and establish the borders of this nation is over, and a more statesmanlike ruler is now needed.

Beyond all considerations of Solomon's suitability, I believe that David sees himself as committed to this outcome. His past actions have cost Bathsheba a great deal: her husband, her first-born son, her reputation. Perhaps that is why he feels bound and committed to her in a way that he has not felt towards his other wives. Yet he destroyed Michal's life as well, and clearly he feels no obligation towards her.

Bathsheba and I arranged that she would go to David to tell him of Adonijah's action, and that I would shortly follow her into his room to confirm it. I know that she spoke to him of his wishes for the succession, but also of her fear of what would happen to her if someone other than Solomon assumes the throne. There is still resentment simmering in the family about her and the tragedy that has resulted from David's involvement with her.

David is not easily stirred these days, but Adonijah's action has roused him. Tomorrow will show us how effective he can be in dealing with a usurper.

Send me your thoughts on this. I value your advice.

Under the mercy,
Nathan

4.03 Solomon Becomes King
Ahinoam (at Jerusalem) writes to her sister Milcah (at Jezreel)

Dear sister,

The speculation about who will succeed David has come to an end. Today Solomon was placed on David's throne. There has been conflict in the family and intrigue at the court, but now it is done.

Some of David's followers had supported Adonijah instead, but that was not to be. Of course, my Amnon as the first-born should have had the throne after his father, but when he was killed, the next in line was his murderer, Absalom. I certainly didn't want that one to have it! Joab's disobedience those years ago in killing Absalom was welcome to me. But with the two of them gone, Adonijah would have been next. I suppose that's why Joab supported him, even though David hadn't named him as his heir.

But today, even while Adonijah and his friends were celebrating his proclamation of himself as king, David had Nathan and some others publicly crown Solomon. I had seen Nathan and Bathsheba around the palace speaking to each other and seeking audience with David, so I knew something was afoot.

The people like Solomon and rallied around to cheer him as he went to sit on David's throne. He is not a warrior like some others in the family, and they expect he will not lead the young men away in more wars. Beyond that we do not know much about him. He has kept to himself over the years, or has been with the sages with whom he studies. He is not often present at the palace, perhaps because many still resent his mother's role in the beginning of David's troubles. For myself, I think more blame lies with the king.

After Adonijah and his supporters heard what David had done, they scattered in terror to their homes. Adonijah went to the altar seeking sanctuary. When Solomon learned of it, he sent for Adonijah and promised that he would not be executed.

Now that this is out in the open, plans for succession can be made and acted upon. David had been reluctant to let go. For me there are no good choices because my Amnon, who should have been king, is dead. But Solomon's appointment is much easier for me to deal with than Adonijah's would have been. David has stepped away from the usual succession of the first-born, and that is some comfort to me. But small comfort.

We are old women now, Milcah, and yet I find that passions do not die. I am still angry at David for his lack of discipline in the family. Had he acted earlier my Amnon might have been saved. When David dies, and I think that will happen soon, I plan to come to Jezreel to be with you. There will be nothing to keep me here.

With love,
Ahinoam

4.04 David Instructs Solomon
Nathan the prophet (at Jerusalem) writes to Gad the prophet (at Ramah)

Dear colleague,
King David brought me into his inner room today to witness a private conversation between himself and Solomon, his appointed heir. There were two parts to their exchange, one encouraging, the other quite disturbing.

David told Solomon of the promise he has had from the Lord that his descendants will rule in Israel so long as they are faithful. David entreated Solomon to remember the law of Moses and to practise all that he has learned about the worship of the Lord. This was encouraging.

But the king then spoke of a few individuals and gave Solomon instructions about them. Joab is to be put to death! The details of time and place were left to Solomon, but David said he wants Joab punished for his murders of Abner, the commander of Saul's army, and Amasa, who had been appointed commander of David's army after Absalom's rebellion. I have wondered why David had not dealt with Amasa's murder himself, but the talk in the court at the time was that he had no other general on whom he could rely if Joab were removed.

Now I am surprised that David feels that at this stage in Joab's life, punishment by death is warranted. Is David not admitting his own motives to himself or to his son? The ills against the family were left out of his description of Joab's guilt. He made no mention of Joab's slaying of Absalom against his explicit command. Neither did he refer to Joab's support for Adonijah's attempt to take the throne. Is David afraid that Solomon's reign might be weakened by having a general who supported a rival? Is this good political advice, even if a bit ruthless? Or does David think he has the mind of the Lord in this as in so many other things?

He also said that Solomon is to treat the family of Barzillai, who provisioned David and his court during Absalom's revolt, as friends and allies. David remains concerned with promises and keeping promises, even though he has in his weakness violated some of his closest relationships.

Finally, Shimei, who cursed David when he fled from Jerusalem, is to be put to death. David had promised not to harm Shimei himself and clearly felt bound by that promise. However, he does not feel that Solomon is also bound by it. Again, is he speaking here as he would think that the Lord would have him speak? Or is it one final attempt on his part to remove the last remaining threat from the house of Saul so that his own dynasty will be unchallenged?

David's voice was weak, and we had to strain to hear him. It was not possible to see how emotional he was over what he was saying because simply saying it was a struggle for him. So I wonder again about this man. Did I see a man of God give instructions to another pious man about how to set right some moral debts? Or did I see a manipulative politician give advice to a ruthless successor? Or did I see both?

I wish that I had others to whom I could speak about these matters. As I grow older, many of my close friends are gone, including many of those who have served the Lord with me here at David's court. I particularly miss being able to talk to Abiathar. He has been hard to find and even harder to talk to since his ill-considered support of Adonijah's bid for the throne. I hope that we will find a way to become comfortable with each other again.

I would value your advice if you can come to visit me.

Under the mercy,
Nathan

4.05 Civil and Religious Arrangements
Abigail (at Jerusalem) writes to her sister Sarah (at Bethel)

Dear sister,
The king has been roused from lethargy by the need to establish his legacy. He has made Solomon king and has been busy with other arrangements. Through the years here in Jerusalem he has

created various offices and given people positions of responsibility. Now he is confirming and expanding all of this. Some of it has to do with government and some of it has to do with the Lord and his worship. And, as always with David, it's difficult to separate the two. He's preparing a structure to hand on to Solomon, and this project has him working as he has not done for a long time. I see in him again the vision and the intellectual energy that excited me when I first met him in the desert.

I would have liked to have been involved in this part of his life, but I've learned not to expect that. I often wonder how our lives might have been different if my Chileab, born in those early years, had survived. Certainly the relationships among the other sons would have been different with another than Absalom being second in line for the throne, and perhaps David and I would have found a different way to live with each other too. Although I'm never sure of that because his other children have not held him close to their mothers. In the end there's no value in such speculation.

David is taking a great deal of personal interest in the court singers and musicians. His own poetry and songs are a large part of what they use. He talks to them about how he thinks about the Lord and reflects that thinking in his writing. He reveals more of his thinking to them than he does to his closest advisors.

He has also been making preparations for the temple, gathering stone, timber, and metals that will be used. He has commissioned Solomon to do this work and has charged the leaders of the people with the responsibility of helping Solomon. He has organized the Levites into groups with various responsibilities around the temple construction and the ongoing care of the place and the worship in it.

I do think this temple is a wonderful idea. It will mark the maturity of the nation. It will be a unifying thing in Israel. It will also draw respect from other nations. Moreover, it will give David and the others faithful to God a place to weave together God's rule and the king's rule.

The king has also clarified the responsibilities in his government: treasury, all aspects of agriculture, archives, and the membership in his council of advisors. This is intended to make the transition to Solomon's rule smooth and to provide him with strong leaders to command. I know David has been giving

Solomon specific advice, but only Nathan is allowed into their meetings and none of the three talk about them.

David believes his end is near now, although he's thought that before. I am pleased to see him putting his affairs in order. He has become again the man I admired and loved. But this man will not last long at the pace he has set for himself. So I will soon be coming home.

With love,
Abigail

4.06 David's Plans for the Temple
Nathan the prophet (at Jerusalem) writes to Gad the prophet (at Ramah)

Dear colleague,
King David today made a public ceremony of commissioning Solomon as the one to build a temple for God in Jerusalem. David has been disappointed that he could not build the house himself, but he has never forgotten the project. His understanding that God would not let him build it because he is a man of war has been a hard message for him. He has seen himself as following the word of God in the various battles that he has fought. If he cannot build, however, he can certainly direct his energy at other aspects of the project.

Today any of us who might have been concerned that Solomon would not take up the task have been reassured. David has made such an open display of the importance of this project that it cannot now be ignored, even if Solomon as king develops other priorities of his own.

David even handed over to Solomon specific plans for the design and furnishing of the temple. These have been made clear to him at God's direction, he says. I believe he is drawing a parallel between himself with the plans for the temple and Moses who received the plans for the tabernacle in the wilderness directly from God.

The king has told me of his hope that his dynasty will be a new thing in Israel, establishing a new relationship among God and his people and God's regent. He says God has promised him that

David's descendants will rule so long as they serve God. So David wants to do whatever he can to ensure the continued service and continued rule of his family.

Under the mercy,
Nathan

4.07 Gifts for the Temple
Joab (at Jerusalem) writes to his mother, Zeruiah (at Bethlehem)

Dear Mother,
Hope for any outcome of the succession that we would be able to support is gone. Today David publicly affirmed Solomon as king after him and handed on to Solomon the responsibility for building the temple of which he has dreamed. There is no longer anything that can be done to dislodge Solomon.

The temple is not only David's private project now because he has handed it on to Solomon. He has also involved all the people in it. He displayed the wealth that he has collected to build and furnish the temple and challenged the leaders of the people to show their support. And this they did; representatives of all the tribes and of all parts of the army gave generously. Now they all have a stake in this.

David cannot last much longer, and I fear that I will be shut out of Solomon's administration. There is little joy here for me.

Your loving son,
Joab

4.08 David's Meditation: Dedication of the Temple
David writes at Jerusalem

> I will extol you, O Lord, for you have drawn me up,
>   and did not let my foes rejoice over me.
> O Lord my God, I cried to you for help,
>   and you have healed me.
> O Lord, you brought up my soul from Sheol,
>   restored me to life from among those gone down to the Pit.

Sing praises to the Lord, O you his faithful ones,
    and give thanks to his holy name.
For his anger is but for a moment;
    his favour is for a lifetime.
Weeping may linger for the night,
    but joy comes with the morning.

As for me, I said in my prosperity,
    "I shall never be moved."
By your favour, O Lord,
    you had established me as a strong mountain;
you hid your face;
    I was dismayed.
To you, O Lord, I cried,
    and to the Lord I made supplication:
"What profit is there in my death,
    if I go down to the Pit?
Will the dust praise you?
    Will it tell of your faithfulness?
Hear, O Lord, and be gracious to me!
    O Lord, be my helper!"

You have turned my mourning into dancing;
    you have taken off my sackcloth
    and clothed me with joy,
so that my soul may praise you and not be silent.
    O Lord my God, I will give thanks to you forever.

4.09 David's Meditation: Prayer for the Temple
David writes at Jerusalem

Blessed are you, O Lord,
    the God of our ancestor Israel,
    forever and ever.
Yours, O Lord, are the greatness, the power,
    the glory, the victory, and the majesty;
    for all that is in the heavens and on the earth is yours;
yours is the kingdom, O Lord,
    and you are exalted as head above all.

> Riches and honour come from you,
>   and you rule over all.
> In your hand are power and might;
>   and it is in your hand to make great and to give strength
>   to all.
> And now, our God, we give thanks to you
>   and praise your glorious name.

But who am I, and what is my people, that we should be able to make this freewill offering? For all things come from you, and of your own have we given you. For we are aliens and transients before you, as were all our ancestors; our days on the earth are like a shadow, and there is no hope. O Lord our God, all this abundance that we have provided for building you a house for your holy name comes from your hand and is all your own. I know, my God, that you search the heart, and take pleasure in uprightness; in the uprightness of my heart I have freely offered all these things, and now I have seen your people, who are present here, offering freely and joyously to you. O Lord, the God of Abraham, Isaac, and Israel, our ancestors, keep forever such purposes and thoughts in the hearts of your people, and direct their hearts toward you. Grant to my son Solomon that with single mind he may keep your commandments, your decrees, and your statutes, performing all of them, and that he may build the temple for which I have made provision.

4.10 David's Death

Heman the singer (at Jerusalem) writes to Gad the prophet (at Ramah)

My friend,
Today King David died.
   An expected death, and welcome in that it ends his suffering, but still there is a huge sense of loss. He reigned seven years over Judah and thirty-three years over all Israel. He lived a long and prosperous life.
   We have great hopes for Solomon as the next king and for the descendants to follow him. And we have great hopes for the construction of the temple that David has planned and of the pattern of worship that will be established there.

The company of temple singers and musicians that David founded will mourn loudly for him. We will make a memorial that will never be repeated, because he will never be replaced. Can you come to be part of this?

Under the mercy,
Heman

5 Reflection

Zadok the Scribe's Commentary

This ends the collection of documents on the course of David's life as seen by those around him. But a particularly interesting group of writings in the collection appears to be notes from a series of addresses that David gave at the end of his life. He had established a company of singers who would participate in the worship rituals. The chief singer was a man named Heman. These notes, if they are accurate, indicate that Heman was David's friend, and had convinced the king to talk about the songs that he had written for the worship rituals. Many of these songs, of course, still exist as part of our sacred collection.

There is no indication of who transcribed these notes from David's addresses. I have assumed that Heman himself wrote them as he listened to the king speak. In fact, although I certainly cannot prove it, I believe it could have been Heman who gathered together the entire collection of documents I have presented here and left them in the temple that was eventually built by Solomon.

In the addresses the king reflects on several stages of his life. He talks about his music and poetry, and also about his life as the source of inspiration for the songs. Interspersed are his reflections on being king and the isolation and other problems that come with that responsibility.

There are repetitions. There are asides and wanderings from the topic at hand. These certainly give evidence of being the reflections of an old man in a relaxed, friendly setting. I have not tried to change that flavour.

David talks about how his personal life and his responsibilities as king can be understood in light of his beliefs about God. Of course, his explanations of the various events in his life for the most part portray him in a positive light, as could be expected.

If in fact these notes are a faithful record of what David said, I find myself unsatisfied by them on several points. I continue to wonder why these documents were not made known by their original collector. They would have presented a more sympathetic picture of David than do the raw, unevaluated stories in our sacred texts.

David's faith did not stop him from making disastrous choices. Even so, he was a different person after the incident with Bathsheba and Uriah than he was before, even though other kings have certainly done what he did with impunity. He turned again towards God, and he seized again of the burden of leadership. Apparently faith does not necessarily lead to perfection or freedom from pain or loss. David's life shows that life is more complicated than many of my teachers thought it to be.

Nevertheless, I pass on what I have found.

5.01 Early Experiences
David speaks at Jerusalem

Our chief singer, my friend Heman, has asked me to speak with you who will be temple singers when my son builds the temple, about the songs that I have written for your use in the worship of God. He thinks that understanding the background of the songs might help you in your singing. He and I have shared many trials and many good times; music and poetry have been bonds between us in all of that. Several times over the years he has suggested that I talk about these things, but his requests have become more pressing in recent months. He knows that I am coming to the end of my life.

I too believe that my end is near, and that is why I have at last agreed.

You will know that this is a new and strange experience for me. I have not talked about my songs or my life to any but a few close friends in confidence. As I have prepared to meet with you, I have been thinking about my songs as they relate to two truths. One of these is my own life and experiences. In some parts of this I see the hand of God, while in others (less comfortable for me to describe) I see my own failings. I will not try to tell everything about my life, but I will weave some parts of it into what I have to say.

In fact, this idea of weaving together is a strong image for me. When I was a boy in Bethlehem, my father had a friend named Eliab who lived nearby in Tekoa. Eliab's family often visited us, and we often went to Tekoa to visit them. My father was a farmer, but Eliab was a cloth merchant. He bought cloth from distant places to sell in Israel, and his shop produced beautifully woven wool cloth that he sold in Israel and elsewhere.

I was fascinated as a boy to watch the weavers. They were so skilled, and their hands moved so quickly that it was hard to follow what they were doing. Threads of different colours were wound on wooden shuttles. The shuttle holding one colour might lie idle while other colours were in use, then be picked up and made use of for a while, only to be set aside again. It was wonderful to see how these rapid movements of hands and the using and setting aside of colours could result in such beautiful patterns in the cloth.

I have often thought that a life is somehow like such woven cloth. Thread of one colour might represent one person who moves in and out of a life, or a place that is visited from time to time, or a chain of related events, or an idea or theme that recurs. An observer cannot know what will happen next – what colour will be brought back into the pattern, or what colour will be laid aside, for a short time or perhaps forever. But in the end, each life presents a pattern that is unique. In the end, the pattern can be seen by many. But while the weaving is in progress, watchers cannot know what is to come.

I am confident that much of that pattern is a result of the hand of God choosing what colours to add and what colours to take away. But we too can make choices that change the pattern. When our own choices and God's choices work together, the pattern is beautiful. When our choices are contrary to what God wants, the pattern is flawed. The master weaver – God – can make something new and beautiful even with the flaw present, but this is an idea for another time.

If one truth necessary for understanding my songs is my own experience, an equally important truth is the songs and poems that have been left for us by earlier generations in Israel. These older songs and poems are perhaps even more important than the details of my own life. They have helped to shape my thinking since I was a child and thus have helped to shape my life – what I believe, what I have done, where I have lived, and so on.

To show how this works for me, I want to use a fragment of a long poem spoken near the end of his life by our father Israel. Moses recorded for us how shortly before his death the patriarch Israel brought all of his twelve sons together – the twelve after whom our tribes are named – and gave them his blessing. To each of the twelve he gave a different message.

The words usually said in such circumstances might deal with the specific inheritance that the father is passing on to his children. Or they might be words of encouragement that urge the children to live in a particular manner. Some of what Israel said to his sons is of that sort, but not all of it. Some was built of images and difficult to understand. I think that he intended it to be so. I suspect he saw traits in each of his sons that would be worked out in the future of each family and tribe. I also suspect that he looked ahead in time as a seer might, to anticipate some of what might happen in each tribe.

When I was a very young boy I first heard the words that Israel spoke to Judah, the son from whose tribe my father comes, as do I. These are the words of Israel to Judah:

> Judah, your brothers shall praise you;
> > your hand shall be on the neck of your enemies;
> > your father's sons shall bow down before you.
> Judah is a lion's whelp;
> > from the prey, my son, you have gone up.
> He crouches down, he stretches out like a lion,
> > like a lioness – who dares rouse him up?
> The scepter shall not depart from Judah,
> > nor the ruler's staff from between his feet,
> until tribute comes to him;
> > and the obedience of the peoples is his.
> Binding his foal to the vine
> > and his donkey's colt to the choice vine,
> he washes his garments in wine
> > and his robe in the blood of grapes;
> his eyes are darker than wine,
> > and his teeth whiter than milk.

Some of the images in these lines were impossible for a young boy to understand. What has always seemed clear to me, though, even from the time I first heard these fascinating words, is that our ancestor saw Judah as taking a position of ascendancy and rule within the family – now the nation – of Israel. Judah's brothers would praise and bow down before him because he would become a great warrior whose hand would be on the neck of his enemies. Outside the family, he would be seen as one who has a scepter and a ruler's staff, and tribute and obedience would be rendered to him.

This twofold message from Israel to Judah about relationships inside and outside the family has been important to my understanding of what God wanted from me. You have heard the story of how Samuel anointed me when I was a young shepherd boy. Saul from the tribe of Benjamin was then king, and had a son who was expected to establish a dynasty after him. Even so, I began to understand that my anointing by Samuel was an event of great significance. I had been chosen as the one from Judah in whom the words of Israel's blessing would be fulfilled. I knew too that this was not something that I would accomplish myself. The anointing came from the prophet of God, and the achievement of these great purposes would be a result of the presence of God with me. Because my father's house was not a major one in Judah, this was an unusual thing to believe. I was mocked by some of my brothers and learned to keep this matter to myself.

I remained in the desert of Judah with my father's sheep for some years after the anointing and had time to think about what it might mean. Samuel had told me nothing. He was for me only a puzzling old man with a reputation for temper, although I expected that perhaps he was only roused when God was neglected. But he certainly did not help me to understand my destiny. After the anointing he walked out of the life of our family abruptly as he had walked into it. It was the words of the patriarch Israel that helped me to understand I would become a ruler in Israel, and all the tribes would recognize me as king. My kingdom would also extend beyond the boundaries of Israel so that other nations would recognize and pay tribute to us.

Of course, it was unclear to me how this would all happen. My sister Zeruiah, in whom I confided, wanted me to force the issue, saying that if I was the anointed of God, then I could act to claim from Saul what I knew God intended for me. However, I was convinced that just as Samuel had come without my seeking him, so the fulfilment of the anticipated blessing would come to me. In fact, I believed that God wanted me to wait for him to act rather than to act myself.

I tried to be ready for whatever might happen. When I was invited to Saul's court, in one step I moved from the periphery of the nation in the desert of Judah to the centre. I made many friends, and in time had many supporters who wanted me to be king. Even Saul's son Jonathan could see that God was preparing both our lives for a change: I would be king, and he would not.

I will tell you now more about Jonathan, something of which I have never spoken. We were young when we became friends. We trusted each other, even though we did not know how the future might resolve the growing conflict between his father and me. I told Jonathan more about myself and my thoughts than I have felt able to do with any other person.

When the king decided to kill me, Jonathan protected me and helped me to escape. But when the rift occurred with Saul, I lost Jonathan and a relationship that was more important to me than any I have had since, including those with any of my wives. When Saul and Jonathan were killed, I lost something that could never be replaced. Perhaps I should say that I lost something I would not dare to replace. That kind of closeness can only come with great vulnerability. When Jonathan died, I suffered more than I was willing to suffer again. We had already lost some of what was between us, because Saul drew Jonathan into his court and away from me. But the finality of that loss when Jonathan died was overwhelming. Even now I feel I have a hole in my soul where that friendship used to sit.

And I knew that for a king intimate relationships must be even more dangerous. I speak here not of physical intimacy but the communion that can occur between two minds attuned to each other. So during these last forty years I have turned away from that kind of closeness with any other person. I have sought it instead with God. When I have sinned I have been separated from him, and that separation has hurt me desperately, more than it might hurt others because God has been my only refuge.

But back to what I was saying. The king drove me away and I was in the desert of Judah again – not as a shepherd now but as an outlaw and a fugitive. Fortunately I knew that country and its people better than Saul did. Saul chased me when he could spare time from his battles with the Philistines, but eventually he was killed by enemies of Israel. I was asked then to become king of Judah. It was seven more years before I became king of all Israel.

During those years the words of Israel's poem sustained me. I had come to understand that God would act for me and that I was not to grasp the throne for myself. In those years I wrote many of the songs I have handed over to Heman for your use. My sense of refuge in God is evident in many of them. Some came out of specific experiences that you know about, and I have labelled those songs for you with the particular circumstances that gave rise to them. Others came from the general experience of dependence on God. Waiting and trusting in God were sources of poetic motivation for me.

Often I have used powerful images, just as Israel did in his lines. After his comments about the ascendancy of Judah among the tribes, Israel uses the image of a lion at rest after the hunt as a picture of Judah among the other family members. Also, after speaking of the ascendancy of Israel over other nations (under Judah's leadership), his image of abundant fine wine – an abundance so great that animals are tied to vines and wine is as plentiful as water for washing – conveys the prosperity of the nation.

I learned much from those days in the desert even while I was being oppressed and criticized. I had many images at my disposal, of the desert itself, and of the kind of actions I saw in my enemies and opponents. These images helped me to understand the great protection that God was giving to me. And they gave me rich material to use in my songs. Those of you who want to contribute songs of your own to the worship should look to your own experience, and to the images of the world and the lives around you.

You might wonder how I look back on my desert experiences – the time when I was a shepherd boy, and the time when King Saul pursued me. Certainly when I was in the desert I longed to be elsewhere. Being chased by the king, in particular, was dangerous and uncomfortable for me and the men of my thousand. But as I look back on these parts of my life, I see that they helped to shape me. And so I do not regret those times. I would not want to protect anyone I loved from the cost of learning life's lessons. Hardship, even suffering, is necessary for growth. Not all suffering, of course, is necessary – some we bring on ourselves. But here is another aspect of God's masterful weaving: even experiences we would avoid if we were sufficiently wise God uses to make wiser those who are responsive to his mercy.

There is more that should be said on these matters, but I am tired. Let us continue on another occasion.

5.02 Becoming King
David speaks at Jerusalem

I regret if my weariness yesterday caused any of you inconvenience or concern. I know it was already past our scheduled time to meet when my messenger came to you. I had hoped until that hour that I would be able to come. However, the rest I had then means that we can proceed now.

In my previous meeting with you I spoke of my own experiences and the ancient sources of tradition for my songs. These two themes come together again in what I want to say today.

When I became king of Judah, my life changed in many ways. One change was the isolation that comes with being king. Virtually no one is unaffected by what the king does, so there is virtually no one to whom the king can turn for independent advice. When I was a general in Saul's army, I could talk about my own problems with other generals. The king has no such natural confidants. A good king seeks good advisors, but they are hard to find.

I was young when I assumed command of a thousand in Saul's army and learned the responsibilities of leadership by leading. I had not been taught to be a leader. I had not realized how much I would become involved in the lives of my people, how much their personal lives would intrude into my concerns because it affected their performance as part of my thousand, how much influence I would have on them. At first I was almost overwhelmed, but I found help from others with more experience.

I also had Jonathan in those days.

But I came to the throne of Judah with no one I trusted to give me guidance or advice. Of course, there were many people, including my sister and her sons, who offered advice! And once on that throne I was again learning the work by doing it. But I was learning without advisors to whom I could turn or friends who stood outside the influence of decisions I was making and who thus could listen to me talk about my struggles.

Perhaps I might have turned to my wives, but this was difficult. I married Michal to satisfy Saul and to establish a bond between our two families. I thought once that we might have a child who could become king after me, uniting the two houses. But that was not to be. Michal certainly loved me at the beginning, but to me our marriage was a matter of convenience, or perhaps necessity. She was a strong-willed woman, with clear ideas of what behaviour was acceptable for a king. Her father had raised his entire family in the expectation that he was establishing a dynasty. She quickly came to be critical of what she considered my provincial ways.

Saul gave her to another man when I fled from him into the desert, but I asked for her back when I became king of all Israel. This was important, not to produce an heir but to demonstrate my dominance over Saul's family. With all of this, however, it was not possible to be close to Michal or even to trust her.

During the desert years I married Abigail. She is a very intelligent woman, and I might have had a very different kind of marriage with her, had I wished for it. But shortly after we married I lost Jonathan, and she had no understanding of what that loss meant to me. I respected her but did not find the kind of intimacy that I had hoped for. I am sure that she would say the same. I am surely to blame in this, because I would not risk again a close relationship like that I had enjoyed with Jonathan. Sometimes this haunts me ... she was so powerful and beautiful that day I met her in the desert, and I wonder what we might have had if I'd opened myself more to her.

I could go on, but you will not need more details to understand the pattern. After Jonathan I no longer opened my heart to those who loved me. Some of you might chosen differently, but this is what seemed best to me. As king of Israel I had advisors on political and economic matters, but no one who was a confidant. Heman, of course, was someone with whom I could share music and poetry. But I did not feel comfortable burdening that friendship with the affairs of the kingdom. In those circumstances the songs and poems of our ancestors became increasingly precious to me. For only in them could I express thoughts, my fears, and my longings. My own songs became very important as well.

I told you that after Samuel's anointing I began to rely on the old songs and poems of our faith as sources of inspiration. Another that was meaningful to me came from Moses, the first leader of our nation. Just as before his death Israel blessed his twelve sons, so Moses immediately before his own death blessed the twelve tribes that grew from those twelve brothers. Here are the words that he spoke about the tribe of Judah:

> O Lord, give heed to Judah,
>   and bring him to his people;
> strengthen his hands for him,
>   and be a help against his adversaries.

I took great comfort in these words when I was king of Judah and at war with the house of Saul. I was convinced that the anointing from God was not just for the throne of Judah but for all of Israel. So I fought against Saul's house, because there was no avoiding a fight, but I was not expecting to come to the throne as a result of killing Saul's son Ishbaal. Indeed, I was pleased when Abner tired of that destructive war, realizing that he could not win it, and approached me to work out terms for peace. He knew it would mean uniting Israel under my rule, but he was convinced by then that this would be best for the nation and the people.

The deaths that forced a resolution were unnecessary. First there was Abner's death at the hand of Joab, and then Ishbaal's murder by his own counsellors. Joab was impatient in this as he has been in many things during his life. He would look ahead to what he wanted and then take things into his own hands. He was much like his mother in this. In the matter of Abner he let his personal feelings get in the way of the needs of his king and his people. I did not see any need to grasp for what I was convinced God would give to me.

I say these things about Joab, as all that I am saying in these times with you, in the strictest confidence. I will soon be gone from the throne, but until that happens Joab is the leader of my armies. He knows of my frustrations and disappointments with him, but I have told him I will leave these matters between us unless he provokes me further.

My confidence in the words of Moses turned out to be well placed. It did come about that the tribe of Judah was brought to his people: I, a member of that tribe, became king over all Israel. The inspiration I had from these lines drove me further, though. After

I became king of Israel I knew that the tensions between Judah and the rest of Israel needed to be set aside. I began this process with my choice of a capital for the nation. As I was from Judah, one of the cities of Judah would have been obvious and comfortable for me. However, such a choice would have caused suspicion among the rest of the nation. They would have thought that I would favour Judah over other tribes. On the other hand, a choice of a city from anywhere else in Israel would have been an insult to my long-standing supporters in Judah.

If God were truly to "bring Judah to his people," it would be necessary for Judah, and for me as the representative of Judah, to be acceptable to all the people. This meant that a capital would have to be found that did not have the disadvantages of being in Judah or the disadvantages of being elsewhere in Israel. Fortunately there was an answer to this conundrum. The city of Jerusalem was surrounded by Israel for many generations, but it had never been conquered. I decided that it would be a good neutral choice and thus could bind the two parts of our nation together. It was also well situated on major roads and so could serve as a headquarters for war and for trade. Further, the capture of Jerusalem would add a valuable city to Israel's holdings and remove a trouble spot in the heart of the nation.

Here is a place where Joab's impetuousness paid off. I challenged him and the rest of the soldiers, offering his job to anyone who could conquer the city. I was willing then, even eager, to have another commander for my army. But Joab took the initiative himself and was successful.

We did not totally displace the previous inhabitants, but we certainly took over the city. Once the court was established there, I wanted to show that Jerusalem now belonged to Israel. The most powerful symbol of our nation was the Ark that Moses built in the desert to carry the sacred articles as the people moved from place to place. The Ark had been in the hands of our enemies, but through God's intervention it had come back to us. Yet it had not become important again in our national life.

I decided to bring the Ark to Jerusalem. At first there were difficulties, but I am sure you know that part of the story. When I succeeded at last, that was important for me as king. By my determination I was able to demonstrate to the people that I revered our traditions and particularly our faith. I was also able to demonstrate that something new and different was happening. The Ark was given new prominence and identity as the focus of national worship. This combination of tradition and novelty helped me to unify Israel; the traditionalists had something to affirm, as did those who wanted change.

Bringing the Ark to the capital was the fulfilment of much planning and dreaming. But all that effort was worthwhile. I wrote a song about that experience. I will tell you how I wrote it.

In part of that song I made reference to the experience of our ancestors in the wilderness before they occupied this land.
I wanted to stress several things by this. I wanted the people of Israel now to see themselves as like those who had gone through troubles and hardships and been rewarded. We had just emerged from civil war and had established a capital and a place of worship in it.

I wanted the people to see that God protected them, as he had protected their ancestors. This made the worship that would take place around the Ark significant for us all.

And I wanted the people to see that the promises given to our ancestors had been fulfilled in two parts: first when the land was conquered, and second when we set the Ark up in the new capital.

It occurs to me that you may be thinking there are two different ways to view all of this. On the one hand, it can be seen as reflecting the goodness of God who brought our ancestors through the desert and us into a new capital with a renewed pattern of worship. On the other hand, it can be seen as reflecting the skill of a king who brings to completion what had been begun so many generations in the past. In my own thinking there is no conflict between these two perspectives. Because I serve as God's anointed king, these are just two different views of the same thing – like looking at a house from the inside or from the outside.

When God's anointed king acts, it is as if God himself acts. The attributes and behaviour that can be seen in the king should be a reflection of the attributes and behaviour of God. Unless the king steps aside from what God intends, the king and God are merged into one. Sometimes this seems a terrible burden of responsibility, and I've not always carried it well! Many of my songs slip back and forth between these two perspectives.

The song of praise I wrote when the Ark was brought to Jerusalem was formed in part by my understanding of my own role in God's plans. And it was formed in part by what I wanted the people to think about as they saw what was being done. Many of my songs have these two faces: one for me and another for the nation.

As well as songs of praise, I have written many laments that describe the isolation and loneliness I have spoken of. This is something I will return to another time, confident that you are listening with sympathy and understanding.

5.03 A Long Reign
David speaks at Jerusalem

Today I wish to talk to you about the most difficult time of my life. I do not mean the most dangerous time. I was in greater physical danger when Saul pursued me in the wilderness, or when I was with the Philistines hiding from Saul. Also, in the very first few days of Absalom's rebellion, I was not in control of the situation, and Absalom could have overcome me if he'd pursued hard. But when I speak of the most difficult time, I am referring to a period of the greatest emotional and spiritual turmoil.

The first years of my reign as king of Israel were full of good things. I prevailed against Israel's enemies. I was also able to do something to honour my relationship with Jonathan. His son Mephibosheth was still alive after the civil war, because his lameness kept him from battle. I brought him to my household and treated him as I would have treated his father, had he been alive. I was pleased to do so, and I think the people saw it as it was intended.

My family was growing, and I took pleasure in seeing my children enjoy peace in Jerusalem and prosperity. I started to think about the future and establishing a dynasty of kings in Israel through my family.

The good times ended during a war with the Ammonites. I stayed in Jerusalem rather than lead the armies. I had grown weary of fighting and of Joab constantly pushing me towards it. As I look back now, and as I have thought about it over the many years since then, I suspect that I was taking too much pride in the accomplishments as being mine rather than God's. It is easy to accept the deference that is paid to the king as if it comes to oneself rather than to the office of the king. Ultimately, of course, this deference is paid to the king as regent of the Lord our God.

So I stayed in Jerusalem and Joab took the army to war. Who doesn't know the disaster that entered my life then? I saw Bathsheba and brought her to my palace and committed adultery with her. I compounded that evil by arranging with Joab to place Bathsheba's husband, Uriah, where he would be killed. Joab did not object. No doubt he was pleased to have some hold over me, knowing things I'd want kept secret.

However, there was no keeping this secret. Bathsheba, already carrying our child, became my wife after Uriah's death. We might have tried to carry off the deception, but Nathan the prophet came to me after receiving the Lord's oracle about the adultery and the murder. Though I then confessed to God, our child died soon after birth.

These events bound me to Bathsheba in a way that I cannot fully describe. Bathsheba was beautiful and desirable, and available if I wanted to take her. But it was not the physical love that made the difference with her; the others were also beautiful. There were aspects of guilt in it, of course: guilt before God, before the people of Israel, and before Bathsheba. But the pain we shared brought me closer to her than to my other wives. The pain in their lives – and I know there was pain – was not something I felt with them, and they did not seem to understand the pain I felt as king.

I know that the Lord forgives those who confess. But I also know there are consequences to failure and disobedience. For me one consequence was a loss of confidence in myself as king and as a father. Forgiveness from the Lord was wonderful for me, renewing my intimacy with him after this terrible sequence of events. Yet I was not able to transform that sense of personal righteousness into a moral authority in my dealings with my family and my subjects. I do not know how others who have been forgiven would see this. Forgiveness is a complicated business.

There is a proverb many of you will know, about the course of wisdom in a household. I had wanted to pass this on as a truth to my children: "The wise woman builds her house, but the foolish tears it down with her own hands." Indeed, perhaps I did pass it on, but not in the way that I had hoped. Unfortunately, what my children saw in me was not the wise person building up the house, but the foolish one tearing it down. Many nights I have wept over what I have done to my children, feeling far from them and their mothers.

My children in turn did awful things to each other. When my son Amnon raped my daughter Tamar, I did not respond wisely. I did not seem to know how. I knew that Amnon deserved to be punished but I too deserved to be punished. I felt myself in no position to act and could not face what might be required of me if I did. Amnon showed no remorse, asked for no forgiveness. I could not understand that someone who could behave that way could be my son, so I turned away from the reality. Neither could I deal with Tamar's pain and disgrace. So Absalom finally took matters into his own hands and killed Amnon. I did not respond to this terrible deed either, other than by banishing Absalom from Jerusalem. And eventually Joab convinced me to bring him back.

But when Absalom returned, he plotted to turn the people against me and support him as king instead. I am sure that my indecisiveness in family matters gave evidence that I was not able to provide the leadership the nation needed. And, it is true, my personal uncertainty was often reflected in matters of state. There was ample evidence that I was not ruling as I had in earlier years. Many followed Absalom in his rebellion, looking for a stronger king.

I fled Jerusalem to save my family and myself. Fighting broke out between Absalom's forces and mine. Fortunately I could rely on good counsellors who aided me by deflecting Absalom from the early pursuit. In the end, my experience as a general and as a desert dweller, and the experience of my faithful soldiers, resulted in our victory.

But in the decisive battle Joab killed Absalom, in spite of my having made it clear that this was not to happen. Having lost Amnon, I now lost Absalom.

Like his mother, my sister Zeruiah, Joab is ambitious and impatient. He is unwilling to wait for the Lord. I had been inactive for the wrong reasons prior to the flight from Jerusalem. But when we were in the desert again I believed God would bring me back to the throne and I would not need to kill Absalom. In fact, I hoped for reconciliation between us. What he had to be forgiven in the matter of Amnon was no worse than what I had been forgiven in the matter of Uriah. Less so, indeed, for I had left the family without direction, and Absalom had stepped in. I hoped that he would ask for forgiveness, and I wanted to grant it. I did not want to see my family continuing to fall apart. I knew there would be difficulties with my wives if I forgave him, but my dreams for a dynasty depended on a son ruling after me.

I felt too that this flight to the desert was like the time early in my life when I hid in the desert from Saul. I had not taken action to kill Saul, and yet the Lord had brought me to the throne. I did not need to take action to kill Absalom, for the Lord would bring me again to the throne if that was his desire.

But, as always, Joab could see no value in waiting. As he had killed Abner impetuously, so he killed Absalom. I have never been able to forgive him. We have managed to continue together but it is an uncomfortable alliance and different from what it was in the early days. I will not tolerate another offence from him.

Men like Joab, driven by a lust for rapid outcomes – especially those purchased with blood – have been a burden to me. I call such men "sons of Zeruiah" because some of them *are* her sons, and the others think as she and her sons do. As I have needed warriors and generals, so I have used these men. But although I was a warrior and a general myself, I have never viewed fighting as the best way to settle disputes.

This is another reason why my killing of Uriah was such a burden to me. I had chosen it as an easy way out of a situation I should not have brought about in the first place. Until then killing was something I could only bring myself to do to the enemies of Israel's God.

To come back to my story, my supporters and I returned to Jerusalem. The pattern of disobedience and rebellion now established was difficult to break. One of my own sons had led a civil rebellion. Another occurred and had to be put down, and there were more wars with Israel's neighbors.

Out of all of this experience came songs. Most, as you can imagine, were laments. Some were in response to criticism or persecution when I had done nothing to deserve my enemies' attacks. Others regretted my own bad choices.

There have been many occasions of the first kind. It is impossible to be a king and not have enemies both outside the nation and within it. But in those circumstances I have always been able to turn to the Lord for comfort. When I have created my own circumstances of distress, however, I have had to recognize that God would be justified in turning away from me. The wonderful thing about our God is that he does not do that.

Here are some lines from one of my laments:

> Hear my prayer, O Lord,
>   and give ear to my cry;
>   do not hold your peace at my tears.
> For I am your passing guest,
>   an alien, like all my forebears.
> Turn your gaze away from me, that I may smile again,
>   before I depart and am no more.

In this song I am conscious of the Lord's ability to see my guilt and his right to recognize and respond to it. I can claim only mercy. I have no right to expect forgiveness or to claim it. However, in his dealings with our ancestors in the past, God has treated them as his guests, giving more than they deserve. I am like them; I can expect God to be faithful to himself and to the patterns he has established in my life as he did in the lives of my ancestors. I can ask his accusing gaze to be turned away from me even though he has the right to look at me in accusation.

I have taken great comfort in the constancy of our God. What many people think of as God's constancy is his righteousness. But I think of something quite different: though I have often deserved something else, God's constancy is his mercy.

I have told you before how songs or prayers from the past have shaped my thinking about my life and the role that God has had for me. I want to do the same today. You will remember that before Saul became the first king of Israel, there were others, including prophets, who gave leadership to our nation. Samuel was the last leader before Saul. His mother, Hannah, was a devout woman who had longed and prayed for a son. When Samuel was born in answer to her prayers, she dedicated him to the service of the Lord. When he was left with the priests as a young boy to serve God, Hannah petitioned God about her expectations for him and the future of our nation. The closing lines of her prayer clearly reach beyond her own son to one who would come later:

> The Lord! His adversaries shall be shattered;
>   the Most High will thunder in heaven.
> The Lord will judge the ends of the earth;
>   he will give strength to his king,
>   and exalt the power of his anointed.

When I was a boy I had heard about her prayer, and when I came to Saul's court it was a subject I often heard the priests and the prophets discussing. As I have meditated on these lines through my life I have become convinced that they apply to me as the Lord's regent in Israel. Perhaps they will apply to all the kings of Israel that follow me, or perhaps in special ways to some. I do not know how Saul understood them.

Saul was the Lord's anointed king, and so I could not raise my hand against him. My anointing by Samuel so clearly anticipated what was to come that I did not view it as giving me the right to slay God's reigning anointed king. I took great comfort in my own anointing and in Hannah's prayer that the power of the Lord's anointed would be exalted.

When Absalom rebelled against me, I was confident that I would in time regain the throne. Of course, this did not stop me from fleeing or fighting, or seeking good advice, but it gave me faith that I would be king again. Absalom was not God's anointed. There was no need to take his life.

I told you that I have often thought of a life like the weaving in my father's friend Eliab's shop. Colours are woven into the pattern as people or places or themes appear and reappear in an individual life. The weaving could be flawed, but a master weaver could incorporate a flaw into the pattern and turn out a result other than what was anticipated, nonetheless a beautiful thing. So God as the master weaver of a life can take a flaw introduced by a person's bad choices – rebellion, sin, whatever you want to call it – and incorporate that flaw into an unanticipated but beautiful pattern.

This is how I see forgiveness. The pattern of a life is made by both the individual and God. Unwise choices introduce flaws. The master weaver can forgive and make a new pattern. I hope that by its end, the Lord will have made a beautiful pattern of my life, in spite of the times when I have been less than the man I should have been.

5.04 Establishing a Dynasty
David speaks at Jerusalem

It has been a long time since I have spoken to you. I thank God that the illness that kept me confined has passed. I want to talk to you today about my strong desire since the early days of my reign to establish a dynasty of kings in Israel. Of course, this is something that is natural for a king to desire. But I believe it is also something that the Lord has had in mind for me from the beginning. He has made promises to me that if I serve him and if my descendants serve him, we will not fail to have a king on the throne of Israel.

This has been the theme of several of my songs over the years. I have spoken to you before about the intertwining of the idea of God's rule over Israel with the idea of God's king's rule over Israel. Beyond this, I have many times thought ahead to what might ultimately be accomplished by a king in Israel. I have not achieved all that I wanted to achieve.

I wanted to establish a temple for the worship of the Lord here in Jerusalem. I wanted a magnificent structure that would become a centre for national life. I wanted Israel to be known to other nations as mature like them, because other nations have temples in their capitals. I wanted to change how this nation thinks of itself. The wilderness wanderings as Moses led our ancestors from Egypt to this promised land have defined our identity. I want Israel now to see itself as established and secure, with a symbol that is a temple rather than a tent. I planned to build a wonderful temple for the good of the people but also to worship my God. I amassed the materials that will be used for such a project. However, God sent Nathan to tell me that I was not the one to build his temple.

The Lord said through Nathan that it is because I am a man of war, and a man of war must not build the temple. I can understand that. God does not want to be known as a god of war. Nevertheless it is deeply disappointing to me. Knowing my son Solomon is not a man of war, I have named him to succeed me and to build the temple after I am gone.

Other aspects of the work of being king are also left undone. Some I have referred to in my songs. In these I have attempted to describe some of what I understand to be God's purposes for the future of our people and for the future of my dynasty. I pray that my descendants will continue to honour the Lord so that they may build a nation before God as he wants them to do.

At one time I wanted to take a census of all the people. This seemed to me a way to capture what had been accomplished during my reign. The kingdom has grown in size and in numbers, and it has prospered. I wanted to get some sense of the scale of these accomplishments. Perhaps it was pride. Perhaps I had begun to think of the growth of the kingdom as my own accomplishment and had not properly acknowledged God in it. I've battled pride all through my life – sometimes giving God glory for what I do and at other times taking pleasure in my accomplishments as if they were mine alone. So God punished me for my transgression, and through me the people of Israel. The only good that came from this was that at the end of the terrible suffering I secured the land where the temple may be built, land where I sacrificed to celebrate the end of God's punishment on us.

These last years have brought other troubles. My son Adonijah tried to assume the throne against my wishes. More importantly, he tried to take the throne of God's king without God's approval and endorsement. I was warned, and quickly moved to name Solomon as my heir and successor. I believe he is a wise man and capable of great things as king. Like all of us, though, he is capable of great mistakes. I pray that God will use him to lead our people wisely and long.

It pleases me to pass the responsibility to one so well equipped to handle it. But it also pleases me to designate as the next king my son with Bathsheba. The pain that she and I endured together has drawn us close in some way. It is not that I share the burdens or secrets of the king's throne with her any more than with the others. But some unspoken bond has grown from our common sin and forgiveness. Perhaps it is simply that we each realize what mercy means.

I have had to pass on to Solomon the responsibility for a few loose ends in the kingdom. There are some who have not demonstrated the support that he will need as king, and I have had to leave these for him to deal with. I am too old to face these issues myself.

As I come to the end of my life, I realize that I have been lonely. The activity around King Saul and his court when I attended him as a boy to play the harp for him misled me. I expected that among all those people there would be confidants and counsellors for the king. I have not found this to be true.

Perhaps I could have made this to be different. I know that some of my wives wished to be closer to me but I was not able, or perhaps not willing, to make it so. I regret this especially with Abigail; she is a woman of great intelligence, depth, and will. And I grew distant from my children after the business with Bathsheba and Uriah, and again after the tragedy of Amnon, Tamar, and Absalom.

When I was young, and King Saul was approaching the end of his reign, God told him to kill all the animals captured in a battle with our enemies. Saul paid no need, and instead he saved some of the animals. When Samuel confronted him about this, King Saul replied that he had saved them to be used as sacrifices to the Lord.

Samuel spoke harshly to the king over this. You know that Samuel has a reputation as one who could be very direct when the occasion demanded it. Here are some of his words then:

> Has the Lord as great delight in burnt offerings and sacrifices,
>   as in obedience to the voice of the Lord?
> Surely, to obey is better than sacrifice,
>   and to heed than the fat of rams.
> For rebellion is no less a sin than divination,
>   and stubbornness is like iniquity and idolatry.
> Because you have rejected the word of the Lord,
>   he has also rejected you from being king.

When I heard Samuel's words to Saul, they impressed me and frightened me as well. What looked like it might have been a good thing was unacceptable to God. Samuel said that Saul knew what God wanted, and doing what God wanted was the most important thing.

We believe that the Lord takes pleasure in sacrifices as representations of the attitude of our hearts toward him. But what Samuel impressed on Saul, I believe, was that the reality of how we are before God is more important than the ceremonies and rituals in which we participate. Those have no value in themselves. It is the reality of how we think that matters to God.

So, as Samuel said, to obey is better than to sacrifice. These words have been very important to me during my reign. Saul turned away from the command that God had given to him. Thus

God turned away from Saul. Because of this, I was made king. God took the kingdom from Saul and from his household and gave it to me and to my household.

My relationship with God has been characterized by great emotion. I have been deeply devoted to him, I have turned away from him, and I have returned with a wholehearted desire to experience his mercy knowing that I had no claim to it. I believe that God has blessed me not because I have been perfect, because I have not, but because I have been fully committed to what he has said about himself. Not all the time, because I have done things of which I am not proud. But ultimately, that is how I have lived my life, and that is the deep belief that has shaped me: God can be trusted.

For most of my life I have been a leader: as one of Saul's generals, as commander of my thousand in the desert, as king of Judah and finally king of Israel. I have found it difficult in many ways to carry this burden. The people often think that the king has absolute authority and can easily discern what should be done. The truth is that the king can only lead with the support of the army, the court, and ultimately the people. And most of what comes to the king is not easy to deal with. Officials or members of the court deal with issues that are less difficult.

This is perhaps one of the reasons that I have been increasingly drawn to reflections on the poetic heritage of our people, and to my own writing, during my life and as my reign has unfolded. Poetry allows difficult and complex situations to be explored, the nuances expressed. And much of what I face as king is complex. There are few simple choices facing a king, choices where a good thing is opposed to an evil thing. Much more often I must choose among competing goods – or worse, among competing evils.

Faith in God does not make difficult and ambiguous decisions simple. No, that seldom happens. Often, indeed, my faith causes decisions to be even more complex because I must think in ways that others do not. But in the end I believe this is a reflection of God's nature. We want him to be simple, but he is not. He is always surprising us, always revealing an infinite richness and mystery. In these situations I take strength from the knowledge of God, from the expression of our relationship to him as the people of God in the poetic legacy of our nation, and from my own expression of my relationship to him, reflected in my own songs.

Music brought me out of obscurity to the attention of the king. Saul held my harp playing and singing in high regard. Music remains a comfort to me even now. This is why I have decreed the establishment of this company of singers. And it is why I have contributed so much of my work to the liturgical pattern that you and your successors will use.

Throughout my life I have wanted to accomplish something for which I would be remembered, something for God. Yet as I approach the end, I am troubled by uncertainty. The evidence of my life is clear to all of you: this kingdom and its legacy, but also the destruction that resulted from my failures. I have taken comfort from the forgiveness of God. But I cannot know the future. My rule has combined a balancing of forces in court, religious commitment, and the establishment of national traditions. I do not know how I will ultimately be judged. Perhaps what you and your successors will accomplish will be my greatest legacy.

5.05 David's Last Song
David writes at Jerusalem

My friends, this is surely the last time that we will meet. My days are almost complete, and I will soon go to be with my ancestors. I have made my son Solomon my successor and given him my last advice. My hopes for the future and for my dynasty rest in him.

I bring you the last song that I will write. My voice is old, so my singing is diminished, as are most of my former skills. Nonetheless I sing it now as my farewell to you.

God reigns with justice, and so should God's king. He has rewarded me by establishing my house through an everlasting covenant, fulfilling the desire I have long had, a desire I believe came from him.

> The oracle of David, son of Jesse,
>   the oracle of the man whom God exalted,
> the anointed of the God of Jacob,
>   the favourite of the Strong One of Israel:
>
> The spirit of the Lord speaks through me,
>   his word is upon my tongue.

The God of Israel has spoken,
> the Rock of Israel has said to me:
One who rules over people justly,
> ruling in the fear of God,
is like the light of morning,
> like the sun rising on a cloudless morning,
> gleaming from the rain on the grassy land.

Is not my house like this with God?
> For he has made with me an everlasting covenant,
> ordered in all things and secure.
Will he not cause to prosper
> all my help and my desire?
But the godless are all like thorns that are thrown away;
> for they cannot be picked up with the hand;
to touch them one uses an iron bar
> or the shaft of a spear.
> And they are entirely consumed in fire on the spot.

Epilogue

Zadok the Scribe Reflects on His Work

These documents I have given you – both the letters and David's addresses to the singers – have helped me to see the complexity of his life and work, but not to resolve it. Future readers may be more able than I to reconcile the apparent conflicts in these documents. And these conflicts still remain. Even in his last song David confronts me with the contrast between how he lived his life and his sense that God has rewarded him by establishing through him a line of kings.

Behind these events of history and personal lives, the hand of God is at work. I cannot, even after much study, provide simple answers to all the questions about David. But I can agree with David that, at least at times, I can see God's presence in his life.

As David says in his addresses to the singers, he learned to live with ambiguity. He knew that many situations facing him were not going to lead to clear resolutions. I think he knew this to be something that would always be true. No amount of knowledge or study can make complicated issues simple. For David, this is because God is not simple. For myself, I would prefer more definite answers and a God who speaks more clearly.

I have spent much time with David's story as revealed in the sacred books and these additional documents, but even now I struggle to understand the choices he made and his justifications for them. He claims to have given himself to the service of God as king. But he did not have a happy life as a result of that commitment. Instead his life was complicated, bloody, and inconsistent.

Do we all live inconsistently, with pain and frustration – but also with the possibility of mercy? I have given myself to the service of God, serving as a scribe and scholar. I have failed to find in my choice the simple satisfaction that I expected and hoped for. I would like to have the confidence in God that David had, but to avoid the price he paid in his life – and in the life of our nation – to have it. Surely God gives mercy and forgiveness to those who seek it, even without having made David's mistakes. Perhaps even to me.

APPENDICES

APPENDIX ONE
Names of People

Part of the richness of David's story comes from the many interesting people who pass through his life. Some of the characters that appear here are mentioned in the original texts, but most of what they say and are portrayed as thinking are extrapolations. Other characters have been created around the periphery of the drama of David's life: friends, family members, and officials who do not appear in the original texts. This list provides summary information about the various persons who appear in the book. Each entry includes a brief description of the facts that are (more or less) to be found in the original stories. Where I have gone beyond the original in my retelling of the story, I have indicated this by italicizing the additional material in the entry.

Some family connections among these people are important. The Bible refers to more members of each of the families below than are mentioned here.

Family of Saul, king of Israel before David, showing children and grandchildren (incomplete):
    Jonathan (son)
        Mephibosheth (son)
    Ishbaal (son)
    Merab (daughter)
    Michal (daughter)

Family of Jesse, David's father, showing children and grandchildren (incomplete):
    Eliab (1st son)
    Abinadab (2nd son)

Shammah (3rd son)
David (7th son)
Zeruiah (daughter)
  Joab (son)
  Abishai (son)
  Asahel (son)

Family of David, showing wives and their children (incomplete):
Ahinoam
  Amnon (1st son of David)
Maacah
  Absalom (2nd son of David)
  Tamar (daughter)
Haggith
  Adonijah (3rd son of David)
Abigail
  Chileab (son of David)
Bathsheba
  Solomon, also named Jedidiah (son of David)

ABIATHAR, PRIEST OF ISRAEL'S GOD This son of Ahimelech escapes when Saul orders the family to be executed and joins David in the desert. During the conflict with Absalom he stays in Jerusalem but supports David and serves as a conduit of information to David. He supports David near the end of the king's life when his son Adonijah attempts to take the throne. *Abiathar writes in his journal and to other servants of God recording events and his reflections. He is at first not sure that God is with David, and throughout his life continues to be surprised by David.*

ABIGAIL, WIFE OF NABAL AND THEN OF DAVID When David and his warriors are fleeing Saul, they provide protection to the flocks of Nabal in the desert. When Nabal refuses to assist with food, David would have killed Nabal and his household except for the intervention of Abigail. Nabal dies soon after, and Abigail marries David. They have a son named Chileab. *She writes to her sister Sarah about events in David's household. She is a person with intellect and will who is disappointed that David does not include her in his life and work.*

ABINADAB, SON OF JESSE Second oldest of David's brothers, he serves in the army of Israel during the battle in which Goliath was the Philistine champion.

ABISHAI, SON OF ZERUIAH   This son of David's sister is one of David's mighty warriors. *He writes to his mother about events in the development of the kingdom. He is usually in the shadow of his older brother, Joab, and like his brothers, seeks advice and counsel from his mother.*

ABNER, SAUL'S GENERAL   A cousin of the king, he is the principal leader of the armies of Israel under King Saul. After Saul's death, Abner supports Saul's son, Ishbaal, as king of Israel, even though the tribe of Judah makes David their king, thus splitting the nation. He kills David's cousin and warrior, Asahel, after an encounter between the two armies. While negotiating an eventual peace with David, he is murdered by Joab, Asahel's brother. *He records his thoughts in letters to his father, Ner, and in official documents. After Saul's death he falls in love with one of Saul's concubines, Rizpah, and writes to her as well. An intelligent leader and an accomplished warrior, very loyal to the house of Saul, he eventually gives in to the reality of David's ascendancy.*

ABSALOM, SON OF DAVID   The son of David's wife Maacah and the brother of Tamar. He murders his half-brother Amnon after Amnon rapes Tamar. Exiled as a result, he returns and leads an uprising that drives David from Jerusalem. He is killed by Joab and mourned by David.

ACHISH, WARLORD OF THE PHILISTINES   A leader among the nation that raids against Israel from the coastal plains area. During the period that Saul pursues David, David spends some time under the protection of Achish and in his service. *His court clerk is named Ira.*

ADONIJAH   David's third son after Amnon and Absalom. Late in David's life he assumes the throne, causing David to affirm Solomon as king. Adonijah fears that Solomon will kill him for his attempt, but Solomon allows him to live.

AHIMELECH, PRIEST OF ISRAEL'S GOD   He works at Nob and lives there with his extended family. David visits him while fleeing Saul, seeking food and weapons. He gives David and the soldiers consecrated bread, normally available only to priests. He is betrayed by Doeg and eventually executed by him at Saul's command. *He records his thought in letters. He is faithful to God and cannot follow the complexities in the deteriorating relationship between Saul and David.*

AHINOAM, WIFE OF DAVID   The mother of David's first-born son, Amnon. *Ahinoam writes to her sister, Milcah, about her life with David. She delights in the excitement of life with David, and in the vigour with which he pursues it, but would like to know more of what he thinks.*

AHITHOPHEL   A member of David's court, he is an advisor to the king. During Absalom's rebellion he changes his allegiance to Absalom. When his advice is undermined through a conspiracy between David and Hushai, he commits suicide.

AMALEKITES   A nation of traditional enemies of Israel. They raid David's party in Ziklag and carry off their families and possessions.

AMASA   The son of one of David's sisters, he is made commander of the rebel army by Absalom and is confirmed in that role by David after David's victory over Absalom. Joab, previously David's commander, kills Amasa to reassume the role himself.

AMMONITES   A nation of traditional enemies of Israel. David's adultery with Bathsheba and murder of Uriah take place during a long campaign that eventually results in the subjugation of this nation. The king of Ammon at the time of these events is Hanun.

AMNON, SON OF DAVID   David's first-born son with Ahinoam. After raping his half-sister Tamar, he is killed by her brother Absalom.

ARAMEANS   Inhabitants of lands near Israel. The Ammonites hire many of them as mercenaries when Israel attacks Ammon. David leaves the campaign against Ammon to punish and defeat the Arameans.

ARAUNAH   Owner of a valuable piece of land on top of one of the mountains of Jerusalem. David buys this land to erect an altar after the pestilence following the census.

ASAHEL, SON OF ZERUIAH   This son of David's sister is one of David's mighty warriors. *He writes to his mother about events in the kingdom. He is in the shadow of his older brother, Joab, and like all of the brothers, seeks direction and guidance from his mother.*

ASHHUR, SON OF ELIAB OF TEKOA   *The eldest son of Eliab of Tekoa. The members of Eliab's family are friends with those of Jesse's family: the fathers, Jesse and Eliab, are friends; the mothers, Jannah and Miriam, are friends; the eldest sons,* Eliab *(son of* Jesse, *named for his father's friend) and Ashhur are friends. The two boys are frustrated by the limitations of life in quiet country towns.*

BAANAH, SERVANT OF ISHBAAL Baanah and Rechab are brothers, servants of Ishbaal, who murder their master to remove him from the kingship of Israel. They go to David expecting to be rewarded, but David executes them for killing one anointed by God.

BARZILLAI A wealthy elderly man who provides supplies to David during the conflict with Absalom. David invites him to return to Jerusalem, but he prefers to return to his home. On his deathbed David tells Solomon to treat Barzillai's family well because of the help Barzillai has given him.

BATHSHEBA, WIFE OF DAVID Though married to Uriah, she commits adultery with David. After David murders Uriah she becomes one of David's wives. Their first child dies as a punishment from God. Another son, Solomon, is born to them and eventually succeeds David as king of Israel.

BENJAMIN One of the twelve sons of Israel (Jacob), and thus the name of one of the tribes in the nation of Israel. Saul is a member of this tribe.

CHILEAB, SON OF DAVID AND ABIGAIL He appears but plays no role in the Bible story. *He is mentioned in the letters his mother writes to her sister.*

DAVID, SON OF JESSE The central figure of the story. He is born and grows up in Bethlehem before serving in Saul's court as musician and warrior. His wives include Saul's daughter Michal and Abigail and Ahinoam. Because of conflict with Saul he is driven into hiding in the desert. After Saul's death he becomes king of Judah, then king of all Israel after the failure of Saul's son, Ishbaal, to establish a kingdom. During his reign he establishes a new national capital in Jerusalem, and the Ark of the Covenant, a symbol of the presence of God is taken to the city as a way of unifying the nation. Later there is civil war, with the revolt led by his son Absalom but in the end David is victorious. He has troubles within his large family during his long reign. Eventually he establishes his son Solomon as his successor. Some of his songs and prayers recorded in the Bible are used verbatim in this book. *His reflections on earlier poetry in the sacred books of Israel and his instructions to the temple singers on his work as a poet are also included.*

DOEG, KING SAUL'S SHEPHERD   He reports to Saul that David had visited the priest Ahimelech while fleeing from the king. He kills Ahimelech when Saul orders the execution and the soldiers will not touch an anointed priest. *He writes to his brother, Ram. He seeks influence and power and is prepared to set aside the religious scruples that constrain others in order to please Saul.*

ELIAB OF TEKOA   Father of a family living in a town, Tekoa, near the home of Jesse's family in Bethlehem. He is an artisan with a shop in Tekoa and periodic business in Jerusalem. Members of Eliab's family are friends with those of Jesse's family.

ELIAB, BROTHER OF DAVID   Eldest of David's brothers. *Several times he corresponds with his friend, Asshur ben-Eliab. Eliab wants to leave the farm for something more exciting but his experience in the army only leads to more frustrations.*

GAD, PROPHET OF ISRAEL'S GOD   He serves the God of Israel at Ramah. He joins David in the wilderness of Judah. Later, he brings God's message to David when David takes a census of the fighting men of Israel. *A student of Samuel, he eventually becomes a confidant of other prophets and priests. His work takes him frequently to Jericho. He receives letters from several correspondents about developments in the kingdom.*

GIBEONITES   People of a small nation surrounded by Israel. Saul attempts to eliminate them. David is forced to hand over some of Saul's family to the Gibeonites as payment for the blood guilt on Israel as a result of Saul's treatment of the Gibeonites.

GOLIATH   A giant warrior of the Philistines, who live in the coastal plains between Israel in the interior and the Mediterranean Sea, with concentrations in five cities. Goliath comes from Gath, one of these strongholds. In a famous encounter between the two nations, the Philistines propose Goliath as a champion, but no Israelite will fight him until David takes up the challenge and defeats him, thus routing the Philistine army.

HANNAH, MOTHER OF SAMUEL   A devout woman who prays for a son. When Samuel is born she dedicates him to the service of the Lord. *David quotes from her song for her son's dedication in one of his addresses to the singers.*

HANUN, KING OF AMMON   This new king of an allied nation spurns David's friendship. David then leads a long campaign against Ammon that eventually results in that nation's subjugation.

HEMAN, KING DAVID'S SEER AND MUSICIAN   One of the leaders of the musicians in the temple, as described in 1 Chronicles 6:33 and the following verses, and 1 Chronicles 25:4–5. *He writes to Gad when David dies. Zadok assumes Heman to be the one who collected the documents offering new insights into David and his reign.*

HUSHAI   A member of David's court and an advisor to the king. During Absalom's rebellion he intends to flee with David but is persuaded by him to stay in Jerusalem to give advice to Absalom to undermine the advice of Ahithophel.

IRA, COURT OFFICIAL TO ACHISH   *A servant of one of the Philistine warlords, he writes in his journal concerning David's visit to the Philistines.*

ISHBAAL, SON OF SAUL   King of Israel on Saul's death, he is essentially a figurehead. Abner, Saul's cousin and general, the real power in the realm, supports him. Ishbaal's servants, Baanah and Rechab, murder him, expecting to be rewarded by David.

ISRAEL   The name Jacob took for himself, later used for the nation formed from the twelve tribes descended from his twelve sons. David was part of this nation. Israel blessed his sons just before his death. *David quotes from that blessing in one of his addresses to the singers.*

JACOB   The given name of the man who assumed the name Israel, later the name of the nation.

JANNAH, MOTHER OF DAVID   *Wife of Jesse, and a friend to Marah, the wife of Eliab of Tekoa. Jannah is patient and wise in her thinking about her children.*

JEBUSITES   The people who formerly occupied the city of Jerusalem, unconquered when Israel entered the land generations before the events in these stories. David captures their city when he becomes king of Israel, and makes it his capital.

JEDIDIAH   The name given to Solomon by the Lord, meaning "beloved of the Lord," conveyed to David by the prophet Nathan.

JEHOSHUAH *A friend of Obed-edom, to whom Obed-edom writes recording his fears when David leaves the Ark at his house.*

JESSE Father of David, a farmer at Bethlehem. Married to *Jannah*. Their other children include the eldest son, Eliab, and a daughter Zeruiah. *He writes to his friend Eliab about developments in his family. He is surprised by the turns in David's life but passive in responding to them.*

JOAB, SON OF ZERUIAH This son of David's sister is one of David's mightiest warriors. He becomes the general of David's armies. He murders Abner when David is negotiating to become king of Israel. Later he urges David to deal with the problem of Absalom, and eventually kills Absalom. David removes him from his position of commander of the armies in favour of Amasa, whom Absalom had appointed. Joab kills Amasa and resumes his previous position. He supports Adonijah's attempt to establish himself as king near the end of David's life. He is killed by David's successor, Solomon, at David's instruction (David cites the murders of Abner and Amasa as justification). *Joab writes to his mother about his life and work in David's entourage. His thinking is shaped by his interaction with Zeruiah. They share a desire for power and frustration with David's choices.*

JONATHAN, SON OF SAUL The intended heir of King Saul, destined to be king until David is chosen by God and anointed by Samuel. The two young men become close friends after David comes to court. Jonathan dies with his father, fighting against the enemies of Israel. *He records his thoughts about David and the relationship between David and Saul in letters to his uncle, Ner. He does not want power himself and sees David as a worthy successor to Saul.*

JUDAH One of the twelve sons of Israel (Jacob), and thus the name of one of the tribes in the nation of Israel. David is a member of this tribe. For part of the story, the nation of Israel is split, with Judah acting as a separate nation under David until he becomes king of a reunited Israel.

KISH, FATHER OF SAUL Though head of the family, he plays no active role in the Bible or in this book.

MAACAH, WIFE OF DAVID The mother of Absalom and of Tamar. Tamar's rape by her half-brother Amnon, followed by Absalom's murder

Names of People 175

of Amnon and eventual civil war against David, are shaping events of David's reign.

MARAH, COUSIN OF MICHAL *A confidant and comforter of Michal during her troubled life. Michal writes to her several times, as does Rizpah after Abner's death.*

MEPHIBOSHETH, SON OF JONATHAN After David becomes king of Israel, he wants to demonstrate his commitment to Jonathan. This son of Jonathan was lame and so was not part of the battles between the two households. David essentially adopts him as his son.

MERAB, DAUGHTER OF SAUL Saul offers Merab in marriage as a reward to the Israelite warrior who defeats the giant Goliath. After David defeats Goliath, he declines the king's offer.

MICHAL, DAUGHTER OF SAUL Michal loves and marries David, but is left behind when he flees into the desert from Saul. Saul then arranges for her to be married to Paltiel. When David assumes the kingship of Israel years later, he asks for Michal to be restored to him as a precondition to the negotiations. Michal argues with David over his conduct while bringing the Ark back to Jerusalem. She remains childless as a result of their estrangement. *She writes to her cousin, Marah, about how David is distant from her in spite of her love for him.*

MILCAH, SISTER OF AHINOAM *Receives letters from her sister about Ahinoam's life with David.*

MIRIAM, WIFE OF ELIAB *The members of Eliab's family are friends with those of Jesse's family; the fathers, Jesse and Eliab, are friends; the mothers, Jannah and Miriam, are friends; the eldest sons, Eliab (son of Jesse, named for his father's friend) and Ashhur are friends. Miriam receives letters from Jannah.*

MOSES A formative leader of the nation of Israel some generations before David. He blessed the tribes of Israel just before his death. *David quotes from that blessing in one of his addresses to the singers.*

NABAL His name is the word for "fool," and the Hebrew text plays on this meaning. When David and his warriors are fleeing from Saul they provide protection to Nabal's flocks. Nabal takes advantage of their help

176   Appendix One

but refuses to assist them with food. Nabal's wife Abigail intervenes and gives them food. When Nabal dies soon after, Abigail marries David.

NATHAN, PROPHET OF ISRAEL'S GOD   Serves in David's court. On occasion he is the intermediary between God and David. *Nathan records some of his experiences in letters to Gad.*

NER   The biblical data about Saul's family is confused. *Ner is taken to be the father of Abner and brother of Saul's father Kish, hence Jonathan's great-uncle. He is a sympathetic and wise confidant to Abner and Jonathan.*

OBED-EDOM   The man to whom the Ark is entrusted after Uzzah dies during the Ark's journey to Jerusalem. The Ark stays at Obed-edom's house until David makes a second – and successful – attempt to bring it to Jerusalem. *He writes to his friend Jehoshuah about his fears.*

PALTIEL, HUSBAND OF MICHAL   He becomes the second husband of King Saul's daughter, Michal, after David flees to the desert. Paltiel objects when Michal is taken from him and returned to David when he becomes king of Israel.

PHILISTINES   Traditional enemies of Israel living in five cities in the coastal plain of the Mediterranean Sea. They raid the towns of Israel that lie close to them and frequently invade Israelite territory.

RAM, BROTHER OF DOEG   *Doeg, who reveals his own aspirations and frustrations, writes to him.*

RECHAB, SERVANT OF ISHBAAL   See the entry for his brother, Baanah.

RIZPAH, CONCUBINE TO KING SAUL   Abner asks Saul's son and the then King Ishbaal for Rizpah as his wife. Ishbaal refuses, and this breach causes Abner to begin negotiating with David and the elders of Israel for the transfer of the kingdom to David. *Rizpah receives letters from Abner after they fall in love following Saul's death, and writes to Marah in sorrow after Abner's death.*

SAMUEL   A prophet of Israel's God who serves largely during the time of Saul. He anoints David as Saul's successor. *A leader among the servants of God, many of whom seek his advice and confide in him, he records some of* his thoughts in letters to his student Gad. David, in one of his addresses to the singers, quotes God's instruction to Samuel renouncing Saul from the kingship.

SARAH, SISTER TO ABIGAIL   Receives letters from her sister describing events in David's household.

SAUL   The first king of Israel, he preceded David in that role. He was the father of Merab (offered to David as his wife but refused by David), Michal (who marries David), and Jonathan (a close friend of David). Saul welcomes David to court as an entertainer and eventually as a general but becomes jealous of him, tries to kill him, and pursues him in the desert. Saul dies in battle against Israel's enemies. A man who is easily angered, he is an effective warrior and reasonable politician but is not particularly religious.

SHAMMAH, SON OF JESSE   Third eldest of David's brothers, he serves the army of Israel during the battle in which Goliath is the Philistine champion.

SHEBA   A member of the tribe of Benjamin from which Saul also came. He leads a brief revolt of the majority of the tribes of Israel against David after the defeat of Absalom. Those with whom he hides kill him when Joab besieges them.

SHIMEI   A member of the family of Saul. He curses David when David leaves Jerusalem during the revolt by Absalom, and later asks David's forgiveness. David lets him live but at the end of his own life instructs Solomon to kill him.

SOLOMON, SON OF DAVID   Son of David and Bathsheba, born to them after their first son dies as God's punishment for the adultery and murder that led to their union. Solomon eventually succeeds David as king of Israel. David instructs him on plans for the temple and worship in Jerusalem.

TAMAR, DAUGHTER OF DAVID   David's daughter. Her mother is Maacah, and Absalom is her brother. Amnon, her half-brother and the first-born son of David's family, rapes her. As a result, Absalom murders Amnon and takes Tamar into his household. *She writes to Zeruiah after her rape.*

178 Appendix One

URIAH   One of David's warrior heroes. During the campaign against the Ammonites, David commits adultery with Uriah's wife, Bathsheba, then has Uriah murdered and takes Bathsheba as his wife.

UZZAH   David's servant and part of the group escorting the Ark to Jerusalem. When the oxen drawing the cart with the Ark stumble, he touches the Ark to steady it and is killed by God.

ZADOK THE SCRIBE   He lives about six hundred years after the reign of David, so does not properly fit the category described in the title of this section. He is one of those involved in restoring order to the storehouses of the Temple in Jerusalem after the return of Israel from a long period of exile from their own land. The biblical text that describes him is Nehemiah 13:13. *He discovers a bundle of documents augmenting the biblical stories of David and arranges them in the form given in this book. He is the designated teller of this story.*

ZERUIAH, DAUGHTER OF JESSE   David's sister and the mother of three of his mightiest war leaders: Joab, Abishai, and Asahel. *She is a strong personality behind the scenes. Her sons frequently write to her for advice. She writes to Joab when she discovers what lies behind David's plan to have Uriah killed. She seeks power for her brother and her sons and is more in favour of aggressive action to attain that power than is David.*

ZIBA   A servant of Saul. After the end of the war between the house of David and the house of Saul, David gives Ziba the responsibility of serving Mephibosheth, Jonathan's son. Ziba assists David in fleeing from Absalom during the civil war.

APPENDIX TWO

Names of Places

The story takes place three thousand years ago in what is now more or less the modern nation of Israel and some of its neighbouring countries. The people of Israel had occupied this territory for several generations but had not subdued all the tribes that inhabited it. At some points in the story there is a single kingdom of Israel; at others the kingdom is split into two parts: Israel and Judah, which occupies the south-central parts of modern Israel.

The Philistines live in the coastal plains to the west and south of Israel, bordering the Mediterranean. The Philistines have Iron Age technology (chariots and weapons) that is more advanced than that of Israel, but in the hilly terrain in much of Israel, the chariots are of little use.

ADULLAM One of the places where David seeks shelter when Saul is pursuing him. David uses a cave here as his headquarters for part of that period.

AMMON One of Israel's traditional enemies, located to the east.

ASHKELON One of the major cities of the Philistines, mentioned in David's lament for Saul and Jonathan.

BAAL PERIZIM Site of a battle in which David defeats the Philistines.

BENJAMIN The land occupied by the tribe of Benjamin, one of the twelve tribes of Israel, located to the north of Jerusalem and Judah.

BESOR A ravine southwest of Israel. Some of David's men rest here while others pursue the raiding party that captured the families of David's party.

BETHEL   A town in Israel. *The home of Sarah, sister of David's wife, Ahinoam.*

BETHLEHEM   A town in Judah. The home of David's family.

CARMEL   A town in the hill country of Judah. The home of Abigail and Nabal.

EDOM   One of the traditional enemies of Israel, located to the east.

EKRON   Philistine city on the border of Judah. The Philistines flee here after the slaying of Goliath.

ELAH   Site of the battle between Saul's army and the Philistines, during which David kills Goliath.

EN-GEDI   A town on the shore of the Dead Sea, used by David as a refuge during part of the time Saul is pursuing him in the desert.

GATH   One of the main cities of the Philistines, Israel's long-standing enemy, and home of the champion Goliath. David seeks shelter here when Saul is trying to kill him.

GEZER   A town to the west of Jerusalem. On one occasion David drives Philistine raiders from Jerusalem to this area.

GIBEAH   A town north of Jerusalem, the home and capital of King Saul. Also on the route through which David drives raiding Philistines back home from Israel.

GIBEON   A town near Jerusalem. Abner and Joab meet and fight here with their warriors. After the revolt of Sheba, the Gibeonites are avenged by deaths of seven men from Saul's family.

GILBOA   Mountains near Jezreel where Saul was killed, along with Jonathan and others, in battle with the Philistines.

GILGAL   An ancient city on the west side of the Jordan River. David is met here by the leaders of Israel when he returns after defeating Absalom.

Names of Places

HAMATH   An enemy region located to the north of Israel.

HEBRON   The town in Judah where David is anointed King of Judah and reigns for seven years.

ISRAEL   Name assumed by Jacob and used for the nation of twelve tribes descended from him and for the land that nation occupies.

JABESH GILEAD   A town in the western part of Israel. The inhabitants retrieve the bodies of Saul and Jonathan from the battlefield. David commends them for it.

JERUSALEM   A city inside Israel, not conquered when Israel took the land from its earlier inhabitants. David defeats the Jebusites who live here and makes it his new capital after being crowned king of Israel.

JERICHO   An ancient city near the Jordan River. *Home of Ner and frequently visited by Gad.*

JEZREEL   A town in Judah. The home of David's wife Ahinoam *and her sister Milcah.*

JORDAN RIVER   An important link between the Sea of Galilee and the Dead Sea. It runs from north to south. It also defines an important boundary between land traditionally held by Israel on the west and by other nations on the east.

JUDAH   The land occupied by the tribe of Judah, one of the twelve tribes of Israel. It lies adjacent to the land of the Philistines, to the south of Jerusalem and Benjamin.

KEILAH   Town belonging to Judah, defended by David against Philistine raids shortly after he leaves Gath.

KIDON   Settlement containing a threshing floor. Uzzah dies there when he reaches out to steady the Ark as it seems about to fall. Home of Obed-edom.

KIRIATH JEARIM   Town west of Jerusalem and resting place of the Ark for many years until David decides to bring it to Jerusalem, the new capital.

MAHANAIM City east of Israel, across the Jordan, where David flees when Absalom rebels, and where he waits while his army defeats Absalom's army.

MAON Town in Judah, with a nearby mountain where Saul almost captures David before being called away to repel the Philistines.

MIZPAH *Ancestral home of David's father, Jesse,* in the land of Moab. David hides his parents here while Saul is pursuing him in the desert.

MOAB Traditional enemy nation located to the east of Israel.

NOB Worship centre where Ahimelech the priest and his family serve before being massacred by King Saul.

PHILISTIA The land of the Philistines, Israel's long-standing enemy, in the coastal plain bordering the Mediterranean Sea. From here the Philistines conducted raids against the westernmost towns of Israel and Judah.

RABBAH Capital of the Ammonites, located to the east of Israel.

RAMAH Home of Samuel, the prophet who serves during the reign of King Saul and anoints David as Saul's successor.

TEKOA Village south of Bethlehem. *The home of the family of Eliab and Miriam, friends of David's parents, Jesse and Jannah.*

ZIKLAG Town in the borderlands between Judah and the Philistine territories. David stays here after seeking the protection of Achish.

ZIPH Town in Judah. The people of this place supply information to King Saul about David's location (at Horesh) while Saul is in pursuit.

ZOBAH Enemy town to the northeast of Israel.

APPENDIX THREE

Sources

opening fragment   Psalm 78: 65–72
1.01   1 Samuel 16:1–13
1.02   1 Samuel 16:1–13
1.03   1 Samuel 17:34–37
1.04   1 Samuel 16:14–23
1.05   1 Samuel 17:1–58
1.06   1 Samuel 17:1–58
1.07   1 Samuel 17:1–58
1.08   1 Samuel 18:1–30
1.09   1 Samuel 18:1–30
1.10   1 Samuel 19:1–24
1.11   1 Samuel 19:11–24
1.12   Psalm 59 (1–17) verbatim
1.13   1 Samuel 19:18–24
1.14   1 Samuel 20:1–42
1.15   1 Samuel 21:1–9
1.16   Psalm 52 (1–9) verbatim
1.17   1 Samuel 21:10–15
1.18   1 Samuel 22:1–5
1.19   2 Samuel 23:13–17
1.20   1 Samuel 22:6–23
1.21   1 Samuel 22:6–23
1.22   1 Samuel 23:1–6
1.23   1 Samuel 23:7–18
1.24   1 Samuel 23:19–29
1.25   1 Samuel 24:1–22
1.26   1 Samuel 24:1–22
1.27   1 Samuel 25:1
1.28   1 Samuel 25:1
1.29   1 Samuel 25:1
1.30   1 Samuel 25:2–37
1.31   1 Samuel 25:38–44
1.32   1 Samuel 26:1–25
1.33   1 Samuel 27:1–12
1.34   1 Samuel 29:1–11
1.35   1 Samuel 30:1–31
1.36   2 Samuel 1:1–16
1.37   2 Samuel 1:19–27 verbatim
2.01   2 Samuel 2:1–7
2.02   2 Samuel 2:8–31
2.03   2 Samuel 2:8–31
2.04   2 Samuel 3:2–5
2.05   2 Samuel 3:6–21
2.06   2 Samuel 3:6–21
2.07   2 Samuel 3:22–39
2.08   2 Samuel 3:33–34 verbatim
2.09   2 Samuel 4:1–12
2.10   2 Samuel 4:1–12
2.11   1 Chronicles 10:14–11:3;
         2 Samuel 5:15
2.12   1 Chronicles 11:4–9;
         2 Samuel 5:6–16
2.13   1 Chronicles 13:1–14;
         2 Samuel 6:1–11

2.14	1 Chronicles 14:8–17; 2 Samuel 5:17–25	3.21	Psalm 3 (1–8) verbatim
2.15	1 Chronicles 15:1–16:6; 2 Samuel 6	3.22	2 Samuel 16:1–4
		3.23	2 Samuel 16:5–14
2.16	1 Chronicles 15:1–16:6; 2 Samuel 6	3.24	2 Samuel 16:15–17:29
		3.25	2 Samuel 18:1–18
2.17	1 Chronicles 16:8–36 verbatim	3.26	2 Samuel 18:33 verbatim
		3.27	2 Samuel 18:19–19:8a
2.18	2 Samuel 7:1–17; 1 Chronicles 17:1–15	3.28	2 Samuel 19:8b-20:3
		3.29	2 Samuel 20:4–26
2.19	2 Samuel 7:18–29 verbatim; 1 Chronicles 17:16–27	3.30	2 Samuel 21:1–14
		3.31	2 Samuel 21:15–22; 1 Chronicles 20:4–8
3.01	1 Chronicles 18:1–13; 2 Samuel 8:1–14	3.32	2 Samuel 22:2–51 verbatim
		4.01	2 Samuel 24:1–25; 1 Chronicles 21:1–22:1
3.02	Psalm 60 (1–12) verbatim		
3.03	2 Samuel 8:15–18; 1 Chronicles 18:14–17	4.02	1 Kings 1:1–27
		4.03	1 Kings 1:28–53; 1 Chronicles 29:21–25
3.04	2 Samuel 9:1–13		
3.05	1 Chronicles 19:1–19; 2 Samuel 10:1–19	4.04	1 Kings 2:1–9
		4.05	1 Chronicles 3:1–9, 6:31–48, 22:2–27:34
3.06	2 Samuel 11:1–27		
3.07	2 Samuel 11:1–27	4.06	1 Chronicles 28:1–21
3.08	2 Samuel 12:1–14	4.07	1 Chronicles 29:1–9
3.09	2 Samuel 12:15–17	4.08	Psalm 30 (1–12) verbatim
3.10	2 Samuel 12:18–23	4.09	1 Chronicles 29:10–19 verbatim
3.11	2 Samuel 12:24–25		
3.12	Psalm 51 (1–19) verbatim	4.10	1 Chronicles 29:26–30; 1 Kings 2:10–12
3.13	2 Samuel 12:26–31; 1 Chronicles 20:1–3		
		5.01	Genesis 49:8–12 verbatim
3.14	2 Samuel 13:1–22	5.02	Deuteronomy 33:7 verbatim
3.15	2 Samuel 13:1–22	5.03	Proverbs 14:1 verbatim; Psalm 39:12–13 verbatim; 1 Samuel 2:10 verbatim
3.16	2 Samuel 13:23–36		
3.17	2 Samuel 13:38–14:24		
3.18	2 Samuel 14:25–33	5.04	1 Samuel 15:22–23 verbatim
3.19	2 Samuel 15:1–12	5.05	2 Samuel 23:1–7 verbatim
3.20	2 Samuel 15:13–37		

APPENDIX FOUR

The Contributors

Abiathar the priest
1.20 Saul Slays Priests Allied with David
1.22 David Drives Back the Philistines
1.27 The Death of Samuel
1.35 David Destroys Foreign Raiders
3.20 David Flees from Absalom
3.24 Absalom Receives Conflicting Advice

Abigail, wife of David
1.30 David Meets Nabal and Abigail
2.01 David, King of Judah
2.09 Assassination of Ishbaal
2.11 David, King of Israel
2.12 David Chooses His Capital
3.04 David and Mephibosheth
3.11 The Birth of Solomon
3.14 Amnon and Tamar
3.22 Ziba Assists David
3.28 David's Return to Jerusalem
4.05 Civil and Religious Arrangements

Abishai, son of Zeruiah
1.32 David Spares Saul Again
1.36 The Death of Saul
2.14 David Is Victorious over the Philistines
3.03 David Establishes a Government
3.23 Shimei Curses David

186   Appendix Four

3.29   Sheba Rebels
3.31   More Philistine Battles

Abner, Saul's general
1.06   A Boy to Watch
1.08   Saul Is Jealous of David
1.24   David Escapes Saul's Pursuit
1.25   David Lets Saul Live
1.26   Abner's Complaint
2.03   Abner Is Frustrated
2.06   Abner Anticipates Success

Ahimelech
1.15   David Finds Provisions

Ahinoam, sister of Milcah
1.33   David Makes an Alliance with the Philistines
1.34   The Philistines Reject David
2.04   David's Family Expands
3.01   David's Initial Victories in Battle
3.10   David Reacts to the Death of His Child
3.16   Absalom Kills Amnon
3.27   David in Mourning
4.03   Solomon Becomes King

Asahel, son of Zeruiah
1.31   David's Family Wonders about Him

David
1.12   David's Meditation: Saul Watches His House
1.16   David's Meditation: The Treachery of Doeg
1.37   David's Meditation: Lament for Saul and Jonathan
2.08   David's Meditation: Lament for Abner
2.17   David's Meditation: Installation of the Ark
2.19   David's Meditation: Prayer for the Dynasty
3.02   David's Meditation: Celebration of Victory
3.12   David's Meditation: Confession
3.21   David's Meditation: Fleeing from Absalom
3.26   David's Meditation: Lament for Absalom
3.32   David's Meditation: Praise for Victory

4.08 David's Meditation: Dedication of the Temple
4.09 David's Meditation: Prayer for the Temple
5.01 Early Experiences
5.02 Becoming King
5.03 A Long Reign
5.04 Establishing a Dynasty
5.05 David's Last Song

Doeg, Saul's shepherd
1.21 Doeg's Aspirations

Eliab, David's brother
1.01 Samuel Anoints David
1.05 David and Goliath

Heman the singer
4.10 David's Death

Ira, the annalist
1.17 David Finds Shelter with the Philistines

Jannah, David's mother
1.03 David Protects the Sheep

Jesse, David's father
1.04 David Goes to the Court of Saul
1.18 David Hides Himself and His Family

Joab, David's general
1.19 Water from Bethlehem's Well
1.29 Spying on Saul
2.02 Civil War after Saul's Death
2.07 Joab Kills Abner
3.05 War with Ammon
3.06 The Death of Uriah
3.13 The Capture of Rabbah
3.17 Absalom Returns from Exile
3.18 David Meets with Absalom
3.19 Absalom Conspires Against David
3.25 Joab Kills Absalom

4.01 Census of Warriors
4.07 Gifts for the Temple

Jonathan, Saul's son
1.07 David and Jonathan Find a New Friendship
1.10 David in Danger from Saul
1.14 Jonathan Protects David
1.23 Saul Pursues David
1.28 A Restraint Removed

Michal, Saul's daughter
1.09 Michal Loves David
1.11 Michal Is Separated from David
2.05 Abner Negotiates with David
2.15 Installing the Ark in Jerusalem
2.16 Michal Is Barren
3.09 David and Bathsheba's Child Dies
3.30 Vengeance on Saul's House

Nathan the prophet
2.18 God Establishes David's Reign
3.08 Nathan Rebukes David
4.02 Adonijah Assumes the Throne
4.04 David Instructs Solomon
4.06 David's Plans for the Temple

Obed-edom
2.13 Retrieving the Ark

Rizpah
2.10 Rizpah Mourns Abner's Death

Samuel the prophet
1.02 Samuel Is Surprised by God
1.13 Samuel Fears Saul's Wrath

Tamar, daughter of David
3.15 Tamar's Suffering

Zadok the scribe
Prologue   Zadok the Scribe Outlines His Project

1.00 Zadok the Scribe's Commentary
2.00 Zadok the Scribe's Commentary
3.00 Zadok the Scribe's Commentary
4.00 Zadok the Scribe's Commentary
5.00 Zadok the Scribe's Commentary
Epilogue   Zadok the Scribe Reflects on His Work

Zeruiah, sister of David
3.07 Why Uriah Died

APPENDIX FIVE

Guide to Further Reading

There is a large scholarly and popular literature dealing with David's era and with the retelling of his story. The works listed here are examples. The reference lists in these works (especially the more recent scholarly ones) are also good places to find further pointers to the literature.

Akenson, Donald Harman. *Surpassing Wonder: The Invention of the Bible and the Talmuds*. Montreal and Kingston: McGill-Queen's University Press 1998.
Alter, Robert. *The Art of Biblical Narrative*. New York: Basic Books 1981.
Bar-Efrat, Shimon. *Narrative Art in the Bible*. Sheffield: Almond Press 1989.
Barrie, J.M. *The Boy David: A Play in Three Acts*. London: Peter Davies 1938.
Berlin, Adele. "Characterization in Biblical Narrative: David's Wives." *Journal for the Study of the Old Testament* 23 (1982): 69–85.
Brueggemann, Walter. *David's Truth in Israel's Imagination and Memory*. Philadelphia: Fortress Press 1985.
– *First and Second Samuel*. Louisville: John Knox 1980.
Campbell, Anthony F. *The Ark Narrative (1 Sam 4–6; 2 Sam 6): A Form-Critical and Traditio-Historical Study*. Missoula: Scholars Press 1975.
Clines, David J.A., and Tamara C. Eskanazai. *Telling Queen Michal's Story: An Experiment in Comparative Interpretation*. Sheffield: JSOT Press 1991.
Damrosch, David. "The Growth of the David Story." In *The Narrative Covenant: Transformations of Genre in the Growth of Biblical Literature*. San Francisco: Harper and Row 1987.
Daube, David. *The Exodus Pattern in the Bible*. London: Faber and Faber 1963.

Deem, Ariella. "'...And the Stone Sank into His Forehead.' A Note on 1 Samuel xvii 49." *Vetus Testamentaum* 28 (1978): 349–51.

Engnell, Ivan. *Studies in Divine Kingship in the Ancient Near East*. 2nd ed. Uppsala: Almquist & Wiksells Boktryckeri A.-B. 1943.

Eslinger, Lyle. *House of God or House of David: The Rhetoric of 2 Samuel 7*. Sheffield: JSOT Press, 1994.

Faulkner, William. *Absalom, Absalom!* New York: Random House 1936.

Flanagan, James W. *David's Social Drama: A Hologram of Israel's Early Iron Age*. Sheffield: Almond Press 1988.

Fokkelman, Jan P. *Narrative Art and Poetry in the Books of Samuel*. 4 vols. Assen, The Netherlands: Van Gorcum 1981–1993.

Gros Louis, Kenneth R.R. "The Difficulty of Ruling Well: King David of Israel." *Semeia* 8 (1977): 15–33.

Gunn, David M. *The Story of King David: Genre and Interpretation*. Sheffield: JSOT 1978.

Halpern, Baruch. *David's Secret Demons: Messiah, Murderer, Traitor, King*. Grand Rapids, Michigan, and Cambridge, U.K.: William B. Eerdmans 2001.

Heller, Joseph. *God Knows*. New York: Alfred A. Knopf 1984.

Heym, Stefan. *The King David Report: A Novel*. New York: G.P. Putnam's Sons 1973.

Ishida, Tomoo. *The Royal Dynasties in Ancient Israel: A Study on the Formation and Development of Royal-Dynastic Ideology*. Berlin and New York: Walter de Gruyter 1977.

Josipovici, Gabriel. *The Book of God: A Response to the Bible*. New Haven: Yale University Press 1988.

Kirsch, Jonathan. *King David: The Real Life of the Man Who Ruled Israel*. New York: Ballantyne 2000.

Lawrence, D.H. *David: A Play*. New York: Knopf 1926.

L'Engle, Madeleine. *Certain Women*. San Francisco: Harper 1992.

Levenson, Jon D., and Baruch Halpern. "The Political Impact of David's Marriages." *Journal of Biblical Literature* 99, 4 (1980): 507–18.

Mazar, Benjamin. *The Early Biblical Period: Historical Studies*. Jerusalem: Israel Exploration Society 1986.

McCarter, P. Kyle, Jr. *I Samuel*. New York: Doubleday 1980.

– *II Samuel*. New York: Doubleday 1984.

McKenzie, Steven L. *King David: A Biography*. New York: Oxford University Press 2000.

Pinski, David. *King David and His Wives*. In Landis, Joseph C., ed., *The Great Jewish Plays*. New York: Avon Books 1966.

Rost, Leonhard. *The Succession to the Throne of David*. Sheffield: Almond Press 1982.
Steussi, Marti J. *David: Biblical Portraits of Power*. Columbia: University of South Carolina Press 1999.
von Rad, Gerhard. *The Problem of the Hexateuch and Other Essays*. Trans. E.W. Trueman Dicken. Edinburgh and London: Oliver & Boyd 1966.
Whybray, R.N. *The Succession Narrative: A Study of II Sam. 9–20; I Kings 1 and 2*. London: SCM Press 1968.